CW00642475

FOR THE MANY

To Keith George
Enjoy!

Mike

FOR THE MANY

PREPARING LABOUR FOR POWER

EDITED BY MIKE PHIPPS

PREFACE BY KEN LOACH
INTRODUCTION BY MIKE PHIPPS
AFTERWORD BY JON LANSMAN

OR Books

New York · London

Published by OR Books, New York and London
Visit our website at www.orbooks.com

All rights information: rights@orbooks.com

First printing 2017

Cataloging-in-Publication data is available from the Library of Congress. A catalog record for this book is available from the British Library.

ISBN 978-1-682191-32-3 paperback
ISBN 978-1-682191-33-0 e-book

Typeset by AarkMany Media, Chennai, India.
Printed and bound by CPI Group (UK) Ltd, Croydon, CR0 4YY

CONTENTS

PREFACE

Ken Loach

It was an election like no other. The establishment, through its press and broadcasters, gleefully forecast the demise of Jeremy Corbyn and his leadership. The old cliche of 'the longest suicide note in history' to describe the manifesto was trotted out with tedious regularity. It seemed that the majority of Labour MPs could not bear to mention Jeremy Corbyn by name. They did not include the principal manifesto proposals in their leaflets and their disavowal of their own party's programme was shocking, not only in its disloyalty but in its stupidity. They were so detached from people's needs that they did not realise how popular the manifesto would be.

Yet, despite all that, the election and Labour's manifesto have become a source of hope for the left, the real left. This was a leadership that inspired enthusiasm and belief. For the first time in living memory, perhaps in the history of the party, the Labour leader supported workers in struggle. Railway workers, steel workers, junior doctors, teaching assistants – all have had messages of solidarity from Jeremy Corbyn and John McDonnell. Unbelievable. Leaders of Labour actually supporting the cause of labour! The Tories and Blair-Brownites shared a collective shudder.

The 2017 manifesto is the mark of the change in the party. Where Blair's slogan was "Labour means business", which, it was soon realised, meant big business, Corbyn borrowed from Shelley: "Ye are many, they are few". Public ownership is now back on the agenda. Railways, the Royal Mail, the utilities and energy supply would be wholly or partly re-nationalised. The National Health Service would begin the process of removing all private contractors; everyone would be employed directly. We would once again build council homes to deal with the housing crisis that has been tolerated by both Tory and Labour governments. The market is rejected as a universal panacea: it will not always provide solutions, as its advocates claim. Where there is a need but no profit, the need goes unanswered.

Most importantly, we would invest with public money in sustainable industries in the most neglected and deprived areas. Security of work and income is recognised as fundamental to all aspects of our life.

There are proposals in the manifesto that reflect our need to live together with dignity, respecting our common humanity and showing solidarity with others at home and abroad. A foreign policy "guided by the values of peace, universal rights and international law" would shine like a good deed in a naughty world. It would change fundamentally our relationship with states with a record of oppression and illegality. The arms industry would suffer the consequences, as would trade, cultural and sporting links with countries to whose human rights abuses we currently turn a blind eye.

A promise to end fracking shows commitment to the environment, in rejecting the use of fossil fuels and in concern for our local landscape. Ending 'punitive' social security sanctions and work capability assessments reflects our revulsion at this government's bureaucratic cruelty to the most vulnerable citizens. The Tories have used hunger as a weapon and forced hundreds of thousands of people to go to food banks. Labour's manifesto shows a determination to end that. The same values are evident in the attitude to education: "a move towards cradle-to-grave learning that is free at the point of use" so that all may reach their full potential.

The section on art and culture should lift our spirits. Keeping open our libraries, providing an arts premium for primary schools and the belief that the arts are not the preserve of a few, but the entitlement of all, echo Labour's 1945 manifesto. Creativity should be cherished for its own sake. This ought to be a rejection of the idea that art is concerned with producing commodities or promoting the tourist trade. Sadly, the manifesto does not make that leap. The phrase 'creative industries', words I would be pleased never to hear again, betray the writer's priorities. Remember William Blake: "Where any view of money exists art cannot be carried on, but war only."

The manifesto could have been bolder in other areas. Why should not all the utilities, natural monopolies, be returned wholly to public ownership? There would be no more private prisons, but why not remove all private involvement in prisons?

It is stated that part-privatisation of probation services has failed but there is no commitment to end it.

Re-nationalise the railways, yes, but why not include all transport for a fully integrated system? Labour needs a policy for the media that deals with the ownership of the press and commercial broadcasting. The freedom of the press has come to mean the freedom of four or five wealthy individuals to promote their far right views. How would Labour change that? It is good to defend public service broadcasting and keep Channel 4 publicly owned but "uphold the BBC's independence"? Since when has the BBC been independent of government or the wider establishment?

This manifesto is a great step forward and these questions should not diminish the fundamental change that it represents. But they are important to consider for the next stage in the continuing struggle for the just society.

There is a further question. The consciousness of this electorate is caught in the struggle between Thatcherite notions of individualism and an objective reality of insecurity in many aspects of life. How can a party that represents the interests of labour, of the working class, present a programme that deals convincingly with current problems but is also consistent with this underlying principle: capital and labour will always be at each other's throats? I hope the essays in this book will reflect on this essential question. Certainly Labour in this manifesto and, it is to be hoped, in the next, has committed to cutting back the power of capital. Is this to be the first stage in establishing public ownership of the commanding heights of the economy? Or is it limited to mini-mising the worst excesses of corporate power?

If it is the latter, then other questions will not go away. In this stage of capitalist development, can we expect to see again strong trades unions? Or secure, lifelong employment, albeit with a variety of different jobs? And sufficient taxes from multi-national corporations to sustain a comprehensive welfare state? If the answer is no, will the party of labour finally confront the implications? And how can the new technologies, central to the emerging patterns of work, be harnessed to benefit everyone, not used to maximise profits for a few while creating a casualised, exploited workforce and yet more food banks?

One thing is plain. Labour will not be able to implement this manifesto without the whole-hearted commitment of its MPs, councillors and the party machine. All of those elements need to change. The conduct of the majority of Labour MPs was de-plorable, politically and personally. They were revealed as being wedded to the ideas that came from Blair's accommodation to the politics of Margaret Thatcher. Attacks from all sides on a Labour government with this agenda will be ruthless. Without a party in Parliament that is committed to its success, it is difficult to see how the programme can be put into practice. That means finding new candidates and new MPs. At the time of writing, that is the most immediate task.

The same is true of the party in local government, where La-bour councils are often excoriated for their implementation of Tory cuts. The party bureaucracy also has to change. The stories of manipulation against the supporters and policies of Jeremy Corbyn are legion and the subject of endless complaints from party members.

Finally, will this manifesto, which has brought such hope and optimism, be a major step in our society's transformation? The answer is up to us, to our organisation, to our commitment but, most of all, to our political understanding. If we fail, the cause of the just society will be set back for many years. But if we succeed, we will have changed history.

Solidarity!

Ken Loach

September 2017

INTRODUCTION

Mike Phipps

Some general election results are surprising, like 1970 and 1992, but 2017 was genuinely astonishing. Labour's result did not just defy all media expectations and assumptions. It reduced Theresa May's Conservative Government to a minority administration. Labour won over 12 million votes, a 40% share of the vote, 10% up on Ed Miliband's score in 2015 and higher than any in the last forty years, except Blair's two landslide victories.

Jon Snow confessed live on Channel 4 News: "I know nothing. We, the media, the pundits, the experts know nothing. We simply didn't spot it."[1] This was perhaps the starkest, although by no means the last, admission of failure from commentators and politicians alike. Precisely why they got it so wrong needs detailed analysis, but the degree of groupthink involved and the convergence between supposedly impartial media outlets, Conservative-supporting newspapers and much of the political class exposed systemic failings in the coverage of the 2017 general election. The dismissive approach to Corbyn by overtly Conservative outlets is perhaps more understandable than that of newspapers like *The Guardian*, which prides itself on its understanding of, and connection to, the inner life of the Labour Party. Evidently, it failed to learn much from its misreading of the two leadership campaigns that Corbyn won in 2015 and 2016.

Lazy narratives about populism, whether of left or right, substituted for serious analysis. But centrist populism can be just as authoritarian, as the post-election trajectory of French President Macron indicates. Blair was populist too in his day, railing against the forces of conservatism, cashing in on fashions for rebranding and technocratic managerialism, celebrating all things new and basking in the inevitability of globalisation, the end of ideology and the triumph of an eclectic postmodernist pragmatism. Compared to this hubris, Corbyn's campaign was less about a populist disruption of the political system than a popular left wing programme that was rooted firmly within its framework. The second lazy narrative was that this was a rerun of Labour's historic defeat in 1983. Michael Foot had been labelled Worzel Gummidge in the media in that election. Boris Johnson attempted to reprise the theme in 2017 by calling Jeremy Corbyn a mugwump.[2] Corbyn was a throwback, a figure of fun, a loser. Only as the Conservative campaign began to unravel, thanks to a robotic, un-empathetic leader and a bleak manifesto that contained nothing for young people and the so-called 'dementia tax' for the elderly, did the mainstream media begin to suspect they might have got it wrong.

Could a leftwing leader win? Surely the received wisdom of the last forty years, a lesson drummed home by Labour's 1983 landslide defeat, and by New Labour spin doctors ever after, was that Labour could win elections only from the centre?

That might have been true once. But all the evidence on the failure of centrism in recent years was available to anyone with enough curiosity to look. It even had a name: Pasokification, coined by James Doran to describe the electoral and organisational meltdown of democratic socialist parties. This was already occurring in Miliband's Labour Party.[3] The collapse of Labour in Scotland in the 2015 general election from majority party to having just one seat was the most spectacular expression of this phenomenon. More importantly, it happened not because Labour was too leftwing, a trope large numbers of moderate Labour MPs lined up to disseminate immediately after the 2015 election. In Scotland, the evidence was irrefutable: Labour had been outflanked from the left by the SNP's socially progressive agenda. Corbyn's success in the 2015 Labour leadership election was a recognition by Party members of this reality. A retreat to Blairite centrism would only accelerate the trend towards oblivion: something new was needed.

This understanding was prescient. The decay of traditional socialist parties across Europe as they struggle to adapt to this new reality is now highly visible. This year both the Dutch and French Socialist Parties were dissolved, with the latter getting just 6% in this year's presidential and 7% in the parliamentary elections. Similarly, the Irish Labour Party got its worst result in history after joining an austerity coalition government in 2016.

Although this crisis may have only recently become apparent, these processes have been gestating over a long period. Tony Benn in his day understood this trajectory and frequently referred to a crisis of political representation, given the similarity of the three main parties advocating first neoliberalism and then austerity. Yet these policies are not widely supported by the public. Privatisation especially, and privatisation of rail and of parts of the NHS in particular, was often pushed through in the teeth of public opposition.

The evidence for this disconnect between politicians and voters was palpable in the 2001 general election when voter turnout fell to 59%, an eighty year low, and again in 2005, when it hit 61%. In contrast, electoral turnout in all post-war general elections in the 20th century never fell below 70%.

Not only was there no electoral expression for alternative viewpoints, they were scarcely covered in the media. Even after his election as leader in 2015, an estimated 60% of 'hard news' stories about Jeremy Corbyn in his first week were negative, compared to only 6% positive.[4] Only in the general election campaign itself, when legal rules about balance were more strictly applied, did this begin to change – which helps explain why Labour could move from being around twenty points behind the Conservatives in the opinion polls at the start of the campaign to being eight points ahead of them a few days after it finished.

The Economist argued in a piece entitled "Jeremy Corbyn, entrepreneur", that Clayton Christiensen's economic theory of disruptive innovation helps explain Corbyn's unexpected election result in 2017. In this model,

> the most interesting businesses start life on the margins. They succeed by spotting underserved markets

4

and inventing ways of reaching them...But as they improve their products they end up revolutionising their
markets and humbling yesterday's incumbents...Jeremy
Corbyn, Labour's leader, spent 30 years on the margins
of British political life...But he spotted the biggest underserved market in British politics – the young – and
provided it with what it wanted: the promise of a new
kind of politics.[5]

There is no doubt that young people in recent years have been
politically "underserved" – "abysmally treated by the British establishment," in *The Economist*'s words, whether over student
fees, house-price inflation or insecure and exploitative employment opportunities. Jeremy Corbyn certainly won the youth
vote, leading the Conservatives by 47 percentage points among
18 and 19 year olds. Furthermore, the enthusiasm generated by
this orientation, the impact on social media and the increase in
electoral turnout (especially in this demographic) to the highest
in any general election in twenty years, helped redraw the electoral map. This achievement unites Corbyn's campaign with left
populist movements like Podemos in Spain. Their slogan in the
2014 EU elections, "When was the last time you were excited
about voting?", could have been tailor-made for Labour's 2017
general election campaign.[6]

Unlike Podemos, however, the ideological origins of the
Corbyn phenomenon were rooted in one of Britain's establishment parties. Some see Corbyn as the natural heir to Bennism,
the leftwing movement in the late 1970s and early 1980s that

reached its zenith in Tony Benn's narrow defeat in Labour's 1981 deputy leadership contest. But this is to neglect the fact that Benn's policies, such as the Alternative Economic Strategy, were specific to a very different time, when Britain's manufacturing base and industrial working class had not yet been dismantled. In fact, the key to understanding Corbynism lies in recognising that it combines much more long-standing democratic socialist values with an inclusive and unifying approach to political practice. Much of this praxis was hidden from view during the long decades of the neoliberal consensus, but there were always alternative roads that could have been taken. The 1984-5 miners strike was a pivotal turning point during these years, not just because of its potential to defeat and even bring down the Thatcher Government – in fact, the miners' defeat definitively ensured the hobbling of the trade unions and set Labour on a path of embracing Thatcher's legacy – but also because the vast scale and variety of supportive action highlighted an alternative vision of class and community solidarity.

Many on the left emphasise the continuity of Corbyn with Bennism, the old left and roads not taken. But there is also something post-political about Corbyn that transcends left and right ideology, offering practical solutions to the new problems in the age of austerity. Indeed, 'common sense' is the term repeatedly identified with Labour's 2017 manifesto, by unequivocal supporters, such as Chris Williamson MP[7] and critics like Tom Gann.[8] Owen Jones too called it a "moderate common sense set of antidotes to the big problems".[9]

This reclamation of 'common sense' by the left is of considerable significance. Stuart Hall and Alan O'Shea have argued that "the battle over what constitutes common sense is a key area of political contestation." For many years, the market was the cornerstone of what constituted 'common sense'.

> But popular common sense also contains critical or utopian elements. For example, there is a widespread sense of unfairness and injustice about 'how the world works' – landlords exploit tenants; banks responsible for the credit crunch expect to be bailed out by taxpayers; CEOs receive immense bonuses even when their companies perform badly; profitable businesses avoid paying tax; and companies do not pass on to consumers the gains from falling commodity prices.[10]

The idea of clinging to such iniquities, and indeed the entire framework of neoliberalism, appears increasingly devoid of 'common sense' and driven by ideological conviction, given the manifest failure of austerity and market-driven solutions to the crisis over the last decade. For Jeremy Gilbert, the 2017 general election was a historic turning point: "neoliberalism no longer presents itself as an unchallengeable common sense, defining a political terrain from which nobody can depart for any distance."[11]

But if common sense provided a basis for neoliberalism to become so dominant pre-crisis, the loss of that status presents socialists with new opportunities. Chris Williamson MP is surely right to argue in his chapter that the left's embrace of this term opens the way for an era of socialist hegemony.

The 'common sense' solutions to the social problems addressed are necessarily radical, because the problems of housing, debt, public health and education, environmental degradation, exploitation at work and many other areas are greater than ever. They are especially intense for young people, for young graduates who were led to expect better, as Paul Mason has argued in *Why It's Kicking Off Everywhere* (Verso, 2011), but also for public sector workers, benefit claimants, frequent NHS users and many other people not identified in the aforementioned *Economist* article.

Those taken aback by the election result also failed to see that Labour's new members, who have nearly trebled in number since the Party's 2015 election defeat, together with their money and enthusiasm, would necessarily entail a changed relationship with voters, if only in the amount of door-to-door voter contact Labour could undertake in 2017. The media seemed collectively to accept that appealing to activists must inevitably alienate the masses – as though the expelled Marxist sects of the 1980s had somehow octupled in number in the intervening years – in fact, for a variety of reasons they went into steep decline – and were waiting in the wings to take over the party. Of course, there were many leftwing activists alienated by New Labour who were drawn back ideologically by Corbyn's ascent, from the Greens in particular. But this does not begin to explain the whole phenomenon. Many of the new intake were wholly new to formal political activity, like the canvasser in the marginal constituency of Hampstead and Kilburn whom I met on polling day, whose only previous experience of campaigning was donning a Corbyn t-shirt and starting random conversations with people on London's vast public transport network about the leader's ideas.

Had the media bothered to investigate, they might have noticed the importance of social media in the campaign, highlighted by Jon Lansman in his Afterword. This should not have taken anyone by surprise, given its critical role in both of Corbyn's party leadership campaigns, as Alex Nunns details in *The Candidate* (OR Books, 2016). One video produced by Momentum, the organisation set up in 2015 to organise Corbyn supporters and drive forward his agenda, was viewed over 7.6 million times and reached 30% of British Facebook users.[12]

One of the key features of the 2017 campaign was the huge number of rallies that Jeremy Corbyn personally addressed. This activity began long before the general election. Ever since his election as Labour leader in 2015, Corbyn was spending as little as three days a week in Parliament and from Thursday to Sunday travelling around the country campaigning, sometimes in places that had never had a Labour leadership visit. In March 2016, he addressed a meeting of 1,500 people in Aberdare, a Welsh valleys town of just over 30,000 population.[13] Most of the media chose to ignore all this, conveniently packaging such unprecedented events into their 'preaching to the choir' narrative.

So prevalent was the myth that leftwing parties cannot be popular that politicians and media alike chose to ignore the evidence of their own eyes – Labour's near trebling of its membership to over half a million, the huge leadership rallies and even the shifting opinion polls – rather than recognise the reality. Jon Snow and others at least had the humility to recognise their collective blunder, but only after the election result had decisively buried the dominant narrative.

The 2017 election was a battle between two competing narratives – a stable government offering a competent Brexit versus an insurgent Opposition, committed to fighting austerity and overcoming the divisions of the 2016 Brexit referendum with a promise of unity and inclusivity. To many, it looked like fear versus hope. These sound like platitudes, but they have content. The referendum campaign a year earlier had seen the stabbing to death of a pro-EU Labour MP by a neo-Nazi, who, according to witnesses, shouted, "Put Britain first" as he carried out the act. Following the referendum, racist attacks rocketed – by over 50% in the immediate aftermath.[14]

It was thanks in no small part to the way Labour fought the 2017 general election that only 6% of people surveyed felt that immigration was the most important factor determining their vote. This breaks down as 9% of Conservative and 3% of Labour voters, down from 47% and 28% respectively in the 2015 general election.[15]

Corbyn's narrative was unifying on other fronts. The Brexit referendum pitted 'left behind' rural areas against urban 'metropolitan elites'. It divided people on generational and ethnic lines, creating conditions where Theresa May felt she could shamelessly pitch for the 'patriotic working class'. Faced with the inclusive themes of Corbyn's campaign, this utterly failed to resonate.

The refusal of Corbyn to continue New Labour themes of demonising benefit claimants continued this unifying approach, ending the artificial division between the deserving and undeserving poor, which Labour had helped perpetuate in the past. One of the factors that fuelled popular support for Corbyn in his 2015 Party leadership bid was the abject failure in the summer of that year by Labour MPs to vote against Conservative Government benefit cuts. Corbyn's principled position on this was reflected in his campaign, which exposed the nonsense that is talked about 'unworthy' benefit recipients, by highlighting how much of the welfare bill goes to people in work to subsidise their poverty pay.

THE DOCUMENT

All these themes were fleshed out in Labour's election manifesto. But this too was pigeon-holed by many in the "appealing to the choir" narrative, not least *The Guardian* which opined that it was based on "Mr Corbyn's preference for energising his own support rather than persuading those outside it"[16] This turned out to be a classic misreading. YouGov found that the manifesto was the main reason people gave for voting Labour. Newly elected MP Laura Pidcock, introducing Jeremy Corbyn at a rally in Carlisle some weeks after the election, described it as "unequivocal statement of hope".[17]

Its emphasis on ending austerity and supporting redistribution and public ownership was popular – in fact polling has shown re-nationalisation has been consistently favoured by most voters over several years, including during the 2015 election. There were plenty of other policies in the document that would appeal as well.

Those who worked on it were proud of the effect it had on the election campaign, in helping boost Labour's vote, energising Labour Party members and engaging the public in a way that few manifestos ever have. It was written from scratch in the space of three weeks from when the election was called. This was a very challenging timeframe. Those involved estimate they averaged 80-100 hours per week to get it done.

It was drawn from papers written by the National Policy Forum (NPF), the labyrinthine process of policymaking developed in Labour's years in opposition, when so-called moderates in charge of the party decided that the best way to move the party rightwards was to replace the sovereign policy-making power of Labour's annual conference with a new structure. These papers had themselves been based on the ten pledges passed at Labour's 2016 Conference following Jeremy Corbyn's second leadership election, as well as two sets of policy documents from the two leadership elections in the last two years. There was a short manifesto consultation process which involved shadow cabinet members, the NPF and trade unions and party members via an online consultation.

The results of the online consultation helped prioritise the policy areas, but it was necessarily limited given the timeframe. "The party does not have a platform capable of involving members in the way that Podemos in Spain does," one insider told me, "but this needs to happen: the NPF is structurally flawed and is not understood by 99% of members – and policy cannot only be made only once a year at an annual delegate conference."

Different sections were written collaboratively between heads of policy in the Leader's team, shadow cabinet members and the executive directors of policy. Almost immediately there were individual one-to-one meetings held with most of the shadow cabinet, and a consultative meeting of the NPF, all ahead of the drafting. Consultations on some specific issues carried on later into the process as policy was still being refined in some areas due to the unexpected snap election.

The costings were continually prepared as policy was developed. "The decision to publish a costings document was taken quite early on in the campaign," one source said, "to demonstrate our economic credibility and as part of our more open approach to politics."

For the many, not the few is an interesting title. It chimed with the theme of the local election campaign Labour had waged a month earlier. Conceptually, it sidesteps the slogan of the 99% versus the 1% of the Occupy movement and appears to speak of class interests while couching its message in populist language. The title was the same mantra articulated at declaration after declaration on an election night twenty years earlier that saw Tony Blair come to power with an unprecedented Labour majority.

But the content of the slogan had changed. Aspiration was still at the core but this was something that could only be achieved collectively. In contrast to the rampant individualism of earlier neoliberal projects, including that of Tony Blair, whose government promoted individual competition and cut social provision, Corbyn offered a very different vision. "We understand aspiration and we understand that it is only collectively that our aspirations can be realised," he wrote in 2015.[18] Insiders confirmed this. "We wanted to present a universalist and redistributionist vision to transform Britain for the many not the few," one told me.

The 2017 manifesto was very different in content too. Firstly, it marked a return to traditional democratic socialist values of community solidarity and social justice. Secondly, it was concrete. There were specific pledges that cut through the usual bland platitudes that are the hallmark of most election manifestos, whatever the party. Even the section on foreign policy, as Glen Rangwala argues in his chapter, had some very specific commitments about recognising Palestine and allowing the Chagos islanders to return to their homeland. Thirdly, there was something to appeal to key sections of the electorate – the abolition of tuition fees, restoring the 'triple lock' on pensions, raising the minimum wage to £10 an hour – real commitments that might be expected to generate enthusiasm among those affected. These policies appealed not just to traditional Labour voters: there is evidence to suggest among former UKIP and Conservative voters that Labour's proposal to renationalise the railways and some utilities resonated as part of a narrative to take back control of Britain's economy from the forces of globalisation.[19]

These unifying themes appealed to voters. If the 2017 election was unusual in that large numbers of voters changed their views during the course of a short election campaign, Labour's manifesto was one of the key reasons for their doing so. The jump in the opinion polls which Labour enjoyed suggests the document altered the course of the election.

But its appeal was not just to the electorate. The manifesto played an important role in overcoming the fractures within the Labour Party itself, not least among the parliamentary party, whose hostility to Corbyn was reflected in their overwhelming support for Owen Smith's leadership challenge to Corbyn in 2016. "It was a manifesto I was proud to stand on," said one Labour MP who voted for Smith in that leadership contest. "It really differentiated us from the Tories and it's the first time I've felt that."[20]

Some have criticised the manifesto for being excessively responsive to single-issue campaigns and activist groups. But this again commits the error of seeing such groups as not only unrepresentative of, but counterposed to, the interests of the broader electorate. To accept this reasoning is to acquiesce to a New Right theory of such organisations as self-interested empire-builders seeking more resources for their narrow agendas, divorced from the needs of a supposed silent majority. Tony Blair's Government reacted to groups largely from this standpoint – even the trade unions, whose millions of members had been a financial, organisational and political mainstay for Labour in its wilderness years after 1979. Jeremy Corbyn's approach to campaigning groups was radically different. It was based on an understanding that such groups, in the context of an electoral crisis of representation, played a vital role in providing alternative channels of engagement that could find an expression in Labour. In opposition, the party had attempted this before, but the long track record of parliamentary support for organisations such as Disabled People Against Cuts on the part of Jeremy Corbyn and John McDonnell, even if it meant breaking the New Labour whip, gave their approach much greater credibility,

The influence of Labour's manifesto can be felt too in the debate that broke out in the Conservative Party immediately after election day. The issues raised by May's critics – public sector funding, student fees, an easing of austerity, were all themes prioritised by Labour's manifesto.[21]

Its impact may be even more far-reaching. Through its concrete radicalism, the manifesto helped widen the Overton window of what can be realistically discussed as potential public policy. If the common sense solutions to Britain's problems are necessarily radical, then all kind of ideas previously dismissed as utopian become legitimate topics for debate, from universal basic income to a shorter working week and more leisure time, ideas explored at length in Rutger Bregman's bestseller *Utopia for Realists* (Bloomsbury, 2017).

But it's not just the manifesto; it's the belief that it will be implemented that counts. Belatedly, pundits are beginning to admire the 'authenticity' of Jeremy Corbyn. But this is not about 'looking authentic', it's about being it, and it's better called integrity. In Corbyn's case, this has been established over a lifetime of political activity. The hard-working backbench MP who never put promotion ahead of principle was the first ever to have a surprise party organised for him by no less a figure than the Speaker of the House of Commons to mark his 30th anniversary as an MP. Corbyn stood on picket lines because it was the right thing to do; he was proved right by history time and again, on Ireland, South Africa and Iraq; he campaigned in other MPs' constituencies even if they were unwinnable, for example in Thanet, which he visited not once, but four times in 2015. All this, and his insistence on not making personal attacks on opponents, built up a reserve of goodwill which helped him secure the necessary number of nominations for the leadership in 2015. It explains why in the summer of 2016, in August, when most politicians (and activists) were on holiday, 4,000 people attended a meeting in a London suburb at five days' notice. Corbyn is not an electrifying speaker like Barack Obama. But unlike many politicians, he means what he says and he likes meeting people. His 34 year record as an MP shows he has the conviction, tenacity and unruffled single-mindedness to deliver his agenda. A few commentators, despairing at Labour's then poor poll ratings, began by 2016 to look for alternative leftwing candidates to Corbyn. But none of those touted from the 2015 intake – and virtually no new left candidates were allowed through under the Blair-Brown regime – had the fibre to stand up to the pressures of Labour's rightwing MPs, its internal apparatus, the media and countless other hostile pressures. A well-intentioned Ed Miliband, elected leader in 2010 alongside a respectable surge in membership numbers, quickly succumbed to such pressures and most similarly inexperienced figures would do the same.

THE NEXT STEPS

Yet for all the excitement generated, Corbyn did not win. Britain is in the hands of an internally divided, unstable Conservative minority government, which historical precedent suggests is unlikely to last its full term. Labour has to look like a government in waiting, but if it is to so, and if it is to win the next election and then transform Britain, it faces a number of challenges.

Firstly, the Party needs root and branch reform. The structures need to be democratised so the influx of new members can play an effective role in shaping policy and selecting candidates at all levels. The Party needs to become a social movement in its own right, a campaigning organisation as well as an electoral machine. The apparatus of the Party will need to be overhauled to become more responsive to the new realities. And the parliamentary party, the source of so much disloyalty, hostile briefing and leaks against Corbyn over his first two years as leader, needs to be held accountable, so that MPs understand that their sabotaging of the possibility of a Labour government will not be countenanced by local members and supporters.

Secondly, a modest lead in the opinion polls is no guarantee of future success. The next general election, whenever it comes, is unlikely to be fought under the same conditions as 2017. Then the Conservatives were complacent and blindsided by the rise of Corbyn: next time they will not be, and the international and domestic context may be very different.

Thirdly, Labour's policies cannot stand still. On a range of issues – from Brexit to taxation, from immigration to constitutional change – voters will expect considerable modification of the ideas that were put together in 2017 in the context of a snap election. It is to the development of that programme that this book seeks to make a contribution.

1. CREATING AN ECONOMY THAT WORKS FOR ALL

Hilary Wainwright

MANIFESTO SUMMARY

Labour will tackle the inequalities in our economy, deliver investment to every part of the UK and develop an industrial strategy to create highly paid, highly skilled work.

We will tackle tax avoidance through a Tax Transparency and Enforcement Programme, closing loopholes. There will be no income tax rises for those on less than £80,000 a year and no increase in personal National Insurance or VAT rates. Nor will VAT be extended to food, children's clothes, books, newspapers or public transport fares. Corporation tax will rise, but small businesses will be protected by the reintroduction of the lower small profits rate of corporation tax and by excluding them from quarterly reporting. Our manifesto is fully costed and we plan to eliminate the deficit on day-to-day spending within five years. Our Fiscal Credibility Rule that government should not be borrowing for day-to-day spending will be overseen by the Office for Budget Responsibility, accountable to Parliament.

We will create a National Transformation Fund to invest £250 billion over ten years in infrastructure. We will complete the HS2 high-speed rail link through Birmingham to Leeds, Manchester and on to Scotland and build a Crossrail of the North, a new Brighton Main Line and Crossrail 2 in London. We will also complete the Science Vale transport arc, from Oxford to Cambridge through Milton Keynes and pursue electrification and expansion throughout the country. In energy, Labour will invest in new low carbon gas and renewable electricity. On communications, we will deliver universal superfast broadband by 2022, improved mobile internet coverage and expanded free wifi in city centres and on public transport. We will improve 4G coverage, invest to ensure all urban areas, major roads and railways have 5G coverage and instruct the National Infrastructure Commission to work on rolling out 'ultrafast' within a decade.

Our industrial strategy will be based on the following measurable missions: ensuring 60% of UK energy comes from zero-carbon or renewable sources by 2030; getting the highest proportion of high-skilled jobs in the OECD and meeting their target of 3% of GDP to be spent on R&D by 2030; creating a National Education Service for England; negotiating a new deal with Europe that puts jobs first; improving procurement; and capping energy costs and investing in public energy provision. Special councils will be established to oversee the security and growth of specific industries and private investment encouraged by removing new plant from business rate calculations. Firms providing local or national government services will have to meet high standards, including respecting workers' and environmental rights, paying suppliers on time and moving towards a 20:1 highest/lowest pay gap. We will appoint a Digital Ambassador to promote Britain's digital economy.

Labour will create a National Investment Bank that will deliver £250 billion of lending power, supporting a network of regional development banks to finance small businesses and co-ops. We will overhaul the financial system, separating investment and retail banking to protect consumers, preventing bank branch closures where there is a clear local need, consulting on breaking up the publicly-owned RBS into local banks and extending Stamp Duty Reserve Tax to cover more assets.

On business, Labour will amend company law so directors owe a duty to employees, customers, the environment and the wider public, as well as shareholders. Takeover rules will be amended to protect workers and pensioners and Labour will legislate to reduce pay inequality. To support small businesses, we will mandate the National Investment Bank and regional development banks to prioritise lending to them, introduce a package of reforms to business rates and crack down on late payment. We will aim to double the size of the cooperative sector in the UK, making employees the buyer of first refusal when a company is up for sale. Labour will bring key utilities back into public ownership, including rail companies as their franchises expire, energy supply, water and Royal Mail.

On energy, Labour will introduce an immediate price cap and take energy back into public control in stages. We will insulate 4 million homes and offer homeowners interest-free loans to improve their property. For renters, Labour will improve on existing Landlord Energy Efficiency regulations and re-establish the Landlord Energy Saving Allowance to improve efficiency. Labour will ban fracking and transition to cleaner fuels and renewable energy. Labour remains committed to nuclear energy and the targets in the Paris Agreement and the Climate Change Act. As part of the Brexit negotiations, Labour will prioritise maintaining access to the internal energy market and Euratom.

***

It's widely recognised that Jeremy Corbyn's success, along with that of Bernie Sanders in the US and Pablo Iglesias and Ada Colau in Spain, is a product of a deep and widespread disaffection – to the point of anger and contempt – with the political class, and politicians themselves. 'They are all the same' is the response that party canvassers hear from every other house they visit. Corbyn, Sanders, Iglesias and Colau are popular precisely because they are different. They do not behave like normal politicians. They are clearly *not* conventional politicians.

This surely goes deeper than authenticity, modesty and an evident commitment to social justice and living out the social values that they preach. I will argue that if movements of the new transformative left which are gaining such support from

those disgusted with the old politics, are actually to be transformative – and not end up either making the same compro-
mises as left governments in the past, or being defeated by the
hostile forces that will undoubtedly face them – then the lead-
erships and their supporters will need to rethink their practice
and go beyond simply a new kind of personal leadership. And
no doubt such rethinking is already underway. I want simply
to contribute to this process, by exploring what it means for
building on the undoubted success of Labour's 2017 manifesto.

First, a point should be made about the limits of a manifesto. A manifesto, like any set of policies, tends to imply the perspective of the architect setting out the plans for the builders to
implement, under architectural supervision – or civil servants
and the state apparatus to implement, supervised by a Labour
government. My critically constructive take on the 2017 manifesto, and indeed any radical manifesto of a left party preparing
for government, begins from a military metaphor rather than
an architectural one. The reason is that where a radical, socialist challenge to dominant interests is envisaged, it needs to have
an eye to questions of the balance of power, the terrain, agency,
leverage and allies, that is, within a framework of strategy, rather
than simply 'policy', as if it could be separated from questions of
agency and the mobilisation of power.

We have only to recall the memories evoked by 'Chile'
and more recently 'Greece', to remind ourselves of the concerted hostile powers ranged against a radical government whose
policies threaten the international interests of capital. The 2017

manifesto might read as if it were no more radical than a re-construction of the gains of Attlee's post-war welfare state, pro-posing a government committed to halting and reversing the last two decades of austerity and planetary destruction and re-constructing institutions to defend and extend the principles of public goods against the insistent imperatives of the deregulat-ed market. But such a project would of necessity be extremely radical and face far more hostile forces than in the post-war world of a mobilised self-confident public and an infrastruc-ture of regulations requiring private businesses to work for a public goal.

POWER FROM BELOW

In this context, stronger forms of state intervention and control over infrastructure will be a necessary condition – including over telecoms, transport, energy and probably land too, but also over finance, turning the banks into public utilities – but it will not be sufficient. The lesson from all, so far failed, attempts to imple-ment a radical industrial strategy indicate that such a transfor-mation requires the exercise of power within production. It may be supported by state intervention, but requires the exercise of power from below, power as a transformative capacity involving the practical knowledge and self-organisation of working peo-ple. This points clearly to a vision of a truly left government as one that enables the transformative capacity and collaborative creativity of workers and consumers to be realised, rather than substituting for it. It must involve a direct transformation of production, not simply more radical forms of redistribution. There are important and very welcome commitments in the manifesto which have exactly this enabling purpose, strengthening workers' existing transformative capacities. For example, there are several commitments to support the growth – indeed the doubling in size – of the co-operative sector, through a National Investment Bank and regional development banks, specifically charged with supporting it, and through legislation to create a proper legal definition for co-operative ownership. Also very important and notably innovative is the commitment to introduce a "right to own" making employees the buyer of first refusal when the company they work for is up for sale.

There are several other commitments to re-establish and extend public ownership which could potentially be combined with participatory forms of control, avoiding the paternalism of the 1945 government. The truth is that the Attlee government delivered its impressive legislative programme of reforms in a way that failed to entrench radical change in the actual social relations of daily life – work, family, community and public provision. Remember the scene from Ken Loach's 2013 film *The Spirit of '45* where, as the flag of the National Coal Board was being hoisted outside the nation's mines to much joyous celebration, the people taking their seats in the managers' offices were – much to the humiliation of NUM militants – bosses of the private companies or senior ex-military personnel. In the

2017 manifesto, the commitment to "in-source our public and local council services as preferred providers" could be implemented through a partnership with UNISON branches, many of which have already had experience of resisting privatisation, with alternative proposals for improving the quality and public efficiency of the service through participatory forms of public administration.[1] Similarly the various commitments to 'Wider Ownership of the Economy' could be carried out in partnership with organisations of labour and of communities of users. But this needs to be made more explicit and prepared for in close collaboration with grassroots organisations, whose practical knowledge and potential power would help to strengthen the popularity and credibility of these significant challenges to corporate power.

It is this idea of developing popular transformative capacity, as part of the process of building support for a transformative left government, that needs more work. This needs to be explored in terms of 'strategy' rather than 'policy'. The notion of strategy would direct us to map – and discover and test out how to mobilise – the resources of transformative power that could reinforce the power that is gained from winning office (always necessary but never sufficient). Such a strategic preparation is especially important given the unfavourable terrain left by decades of neoliberal austerity: the destruction of much of industry; an economy dominated by finance, resulting in devastating geographic and class inequalities; a democracy with its everyday substance hollowed out by privatisation, by the

ruthless weakening of the trade union movement and destruction of workers' rights and by significant attacks on the rights of
women, homosexuals, black people and people with disabilities.

On the other hand, new resources and potential allies are
emerging as a result of great social movements that have grown
up in recent decades contesting global corporate power in almost every sphere of life, from birth control, through education, food, water, transport, waste, wages, trade, the economy,
technology and the future of the planet. What is distinctive
about these social movements is that they have become a sphere
of civil economic alternatives, consisting of more or less autonomous productive initiatives – co-operatives, social enterprises
and networks of enterprises, projects and individuals, especially
in the information and communication technologies that are
at the heart of contemporary capitalism – pursuing values and
ideas born of resistance to neoliberalism and likely to share the
goals of a transformative left government. I would argue that
future Labour Party strategy, with the help of local branches
of Momentum, the co-operative movement and radical trade
union branches, should map the transformative potential of this
hybrid civil economy and consider how it can be strengthened,
including through closer alliances with the labour movement,
to prepare for the new opportunities that a left government
might open up. For example, the manifesto's commitment to a
"right of ownership", giving workers first rights to buy a company up for sale, is going to be more meaningful if workers have
been able to develop their own alternative plans for the future of

the company. Such a process could benefit from learning from and collaborating with economic projects that have been directly concerned with creative alternatives, for example, in relation to renewable energy or organic foods. A workers' takeover of a conventional food company could strengthen a chain for healthy, organic and fair trade food which in turn could be further extended through the value-driven policies for public procurement at all levels – local as much as national – proposed by the manifesto. One way of putting this is that whereas the manifesto includes several (albeit insufficient) institutional forms by which 'the many' – citizens as knowledgeable economic actors, whether workers, would-be workers, consumers, service users and communities – can be agents of industrial transformation, it says little, except in the section dealing with renewable energies, about changes in the content – the 'use value' to use Marxist shorthand – of production. A serious omission, for instance, and a step backwards from a commitment Corbyn made during his initial campaign to be leader, is the Arms Conversion or Defence Diversification Agency that Corbyn spelt out in convincing details in speeches in 2015. In this example, he presented a vision of a process of economic democracy through which 'the many' – through the practical knowledge and social anti-militaristic values of workers and communities – could shape a transition from an economy in which military production dominated manufacturing to an economy in which all the resources and creativity locked into military production were liberated for socially useful purposes.

LEARNING FROM HISTORY

Moreover, this innovative alternative already has a history and international experiences from which to learn. Indeed Corbyn, in his speeches on this, referred to plan for socially useful production drawn up by the Lucas Aerospace workers in the 1970s as evidence of workers' capacity collaboratively to control the uses to which investment and productive capacity should be put and to use the experience as a model for the promised Arms Conversion Agency. The Lucas workers were resisting redundancies and factory closures while at the same time refusing to continue making components for military planes. They provide an exemplary case of the exercise of workers' transformative capacity and the potential power this could create, if supported by a government whose strategy for change was not to presume that governmental office alone gave it the power needed to change the purpose of production and the direction of investment. In the end this prefigurative alternative, despite widespread support, was blocked by Lucas management defending its prerogatives, by a Labour government defending its monopoly of politics and by a trade union leadership threatened by the multi-union unity and political consciousness of its shop floor activists. But its legacy lives on and as new generations challenge the destructive logic of corporate-driven production, the idea continues to appeal of working with those who have inside knowledge of production – indeed the designers and skilled engineers on whom production depends – to reverse the dominant direction imposed by government and management.

So the issue of the agents of a transition towards a low-carbon economy and an economy working for the many, not the warmongering few, is a central one. It is one which needs to be addressed not simply when Labour ministers arrive in their departments – only to be faced with permanent civil servants who present them with options that take for granted the existing priorities of production.

The problem however, reflected perhaps in the relative weakness of the manifesto on the means of workers' participation in the development and the implementation of its otherwise radical industrial strategy, is the fact that trade union organisation in what's left of industry is weak compared to the 1970s. In that era, the Lucas Aerospace Combine Committee – all twenty to thirty of them – crowded into Tony Benn's office in the Department of Industry to discuss the nationalisation of aerospace and ended up exploring the idea of their own plan for Lucas Aerospace. At that time, not only were a very much higher proportion of workers in unions, but workplace trade union organisations in manufacturing were very well organised. This organisation ran across craft and general unions and across office and factory floor, so that the joint shop stewards committees of a factory – and then increasingly across factories covering a whole multi-plant corporation – collectively knew as much about the whole production process as management, and probably more. Their collective practical knowledge of the overview of production and their organised presence at every point in a production flow whose smooth operation depended on them, gave them great leverage. As a result they had considerable collective self-confidence as workers. The idea of workers' control was not strange and Tony Benn's radical industrial strategy saw workers playing an essential role. It proposed an explicit collaboration between government and organised labour, through planning agreements that were intended as a process of negotiation between management, unions – including the shop floor and office representatives of the company concerned – and government. Furthermore, they were to be a condition of government aid. So important were the workers intended to be in this process that Benn, Stuart Holland, Judith Hart and others involved in this policy spent a lot of time meeting large numbers of shop stewards in engineering centres such as Tyneside and Coventry, encouraging them to prepare for this process. In one case, which I observed in Tyneside where I was working at the time, the shop stewards in shipbuilding produced their own proposals, headlined 'Workers' control with management participation' – a sign of the times. Interestingly, these preparatory meetings across the country were facilitated by the Institute of Workers Control, an independent educational and research organisation with close links to Tony Benn, his network of left MPs, Constituency Labour Parties and also the left in the major unions. Could Momentum play a similar role now?

ORGANISING TODAY

Such a preparatory process now would have to be very different in terms of the constituencies that it would need to reach out to. There are no longer the well organised, company-wide, industry-wide shop stewards organisations confident in their capacities effectively to run industry. However, the unions retain a strength in key strategic areas of the economy, especially concerning logistics. Unite has recognised this by creating a dedicated 'Leverage and Organisation' department. This department can claim several important victories, for example over Crossrail, partly because of the way that it combines traditional industrial action with tactics learnt from new direct action movements. One of these is UK Uncut, which used direct action street theatre tactics to focus attention on tax evasion, by occupying the shops of companies that evaded tax, sometimes turning them into hospitals, libraries or other public services for the day.

The state of trade union organisation does not remain static. To survive, unions need members and at the same time workers have begun to refuse the indignities of neoliberalism, such as zero hour contracts, with strikes like that of McDonald's workers and bargaining efforts like those of the GMB, forcing Uber to treat its drivers as employees. Such precarious workers have been part of the Corbyn 'surge'. This is recognised in the manifesto with an impressive list of measures in the section on "A Fair Deal at Work" that will shift the balance in favour of trade unions and labour, but in a way which recognises their role in ensuring industrial development in the public good. Indeed I would argue that the combination of a commitment to a new deal at work with an industrial strategy that includes new rights of workers over production overcomes the traditional divide between politics and economics. This divide is ultimately what defeated the transformative economics of those like the Institute of Workers Control and Tony Benn, who put it on to the agenda but never gained the possibility of leading the party.

Already the new leadership is providing a platform for initiatives, often local, that focus on public procurement and the use of public funds to improve the conditions and the power of labour. This both prefigures in the present what would be possible on a far larger scale through government and also begins to shift the balance of power towards labour. Examples are spreading of civil and local initiatives of this kind, not as naïve attempts to create islands of socialism, but initiatives that go beyond single enterprises. Several trends are especially notable: in particular, opposition to the socially destructive impact of global markets; challenges to the values and design of the technologies now destroying the foundations of human and animal life; the pervasive impact and potential of the new information and communication technologies, and the centrality of how and by whom they are controlled.

The new politics of the Corbyn leadership and of Momentum already indicates an alertness to these new grassroots alternatives. Momentum's importance is that its roots lie at least in part in this civil economy.

CONCLUSION

Alex Nunns, author of the most authoritative description of Jeremy Corbyn's 'improbable path to power', comments that it is

Corbyn's participatory ethos, rather than the specific detail of policies, that

> was really the essence of Corbyn's entire campaign. For disempowered party members in particular, it was the reason Corbyn was so appealing. He was offering them empowerment, and there was no mistaking the message – every aspect of Corbyn's candidacy, from his own selfless demeanour to the specific form of rail nationalisation he was proposing, was about inviting people to take part.[2]

If Labour is to make this appeal to the strong desire for 'new politics' the basis of its preparation for government, and if a Corbyn government is to fulfil the transformative potential of the movement behind it and be able to withstand the multiple pressures of capital, a future manifesto has to go beyond a return to the settlement of 1945. It has to be part of a strategy to stimulate new productive sources of transformative power and in particular to strengthen those alternatives that have been created out of the resistance to neoliberalism.

2. NEGOTIATING BREXIT

Ewa Jasiewicz

MANIFESTO SUMMARY

Labour accepts the referendum result and will build a close
new relationship with the EU, prioritising jobs, living and environmental standards, with Parliament given a meaningful
role throughout negotiations. Fresh negotiating priorities will
be drawn up, strongly emphasising retaining the benefits of the
Single Market and the Customs Union. Labour will immediately
guarantee existing rights for all EU nationals living in Britain and
seek reciprocal rights for UK citizens in the EU.

Labour rejects the idea of leaving the EU without a deal. We
will work constructively with the EU on climate change, refugees
and counter-terrorism. To ensure the UK maintains its leading
research role, we will seek to remain part of the Horizon 2020
and its successor programmes, as well as Euratom, the European Medicines Agency and the Erasmus scheme. Labour will
secure continued EU market access for farmers and food pro-
ducers, protecting them from external undercutting. We will replace the Conservatives' Great Repeal Bill with an EU Rights and

Protections Bill to ensure worker, environmental and consumer rights and equality law are safeguarded. We will introduce legislation to ensure there are no gaps in national security or criminal justice arrangements after Brexit. We will seek continued membership of Europol, Eurojust and the European arrest Warrant arrangements. To ensure a deal that delivers for all regions, Labour will devolve all relevant powers. No region will be affected by a withdrawal of EU funding for the lifetime of the new Parliament. There will be no hard border in Northern Ireland and no change to the status of Gibraltar.

Freedom of movement will end, but Labour will develop fair immigration rules. We will end indefinite detention, distinguish between migrant labour and family attachment and continue to support the work of the Forced Marriage Unit. We will replace income thresholds with a prohibition on recourse to public funds. A new migration management system is needed, based on our economic needs, balancing controls with existing entitlements. We will protect those already working here, raising skill levels and taking decisive action against the exploitation of migrant labour, stopping overseas-only recruitment practices, strengthening inspections and increasing prosecutions of employers evading the minimum wage. Labour will reinstate the Migrant Impact Fund and the rights of migrant domestic workers. We will review current arrangements for housing and dispersing refugees. We will not include international students in immigration statistics, but will crack down on fake colleges.

A Labour government will boost jobs and investment, setting out our priorities in a White Paper and building on our Just Trade Initiative to remove trade barriers and strengthen standards. We are committed to the World Trade Organisation and will rejoin the Government Procurement Initiative, building human rights and social justice into our trade policy and working to prevent the dumping of state-subsidised goods onto our markets. Labour will champion the export interests of SMEs and will ring fence Tradeshow Access Programme grants to help them. We will use a full range of mechanisms to boost British exports, promoted by a network of regional trade and investment champions. We are committed to the digital economy and international negotiations towards an Environmental Goods Agreement at the WTO. We will develop capital investment schemes to encourage inward investment, reviewing our investment treaties and opposing parallel investor-state dispute systems for multinationals.

***

How do you analyse a moment, which was part of a process that is about everything, but was reduced to a yes – no decision? The EU referendum vote was both a mass participatory and mass exclusionary moment. This vote, and Brexit as a whole, can be described as a polarising conflict of marginalisations. The conflict exposed by the EU referendum constitutes an important point of entry into addressing the unmet needs and enabling the de-marginalisation of people who have been living violent marginalisation for generations.

Following the vote, there was a 100% rise in racist incidents. One in five BAME people in the UK reported being racially abused.[1] This is in a context of police impunity for over 1,500 deaths in custody since 1990 within which BME people are over-represented, and with black people in the UK three times more likely to be arrested than their white counterparts, and 44 times more likely to be detained under the Mental Health Act.[2] Negotiating Brexit cannot be understood as a technical, economic process alone but one of navigating and overcoming the lived experiences of oppression in the UK.

In my analysis of Labour's plans for Brexit, I will look primarily at workplace and immigration policy. I will argue that the implications of a "managed migration" policy – including "employer sponsorship, work permits, visa regulations or a tailored mix of all these which works for the many, not the few" – is contradictory and will ultimately work for the few and not the many.

This policy risks reproducing more complex systems of class subordination and fragmentation. Multi-tiered workforces and the creation of multiple statuses with differentiated access to resources and rights put collective bargaining, on a workplace or social level, at a serious practical and moral disadvantage.

The consequences of this architecture of multiple marginalisations exists in a context of manufactured resource scarcity. The legacy and perpetuation of these marginalisations in a future climate change context of *genuine* resource scarcity deserves urgent attention but is outside the scope of this chapter. But it should be understood that a Conservative-led Brexit will marginalise the climate crisis – already evident with support for fracking – in the name of a national interest based on a fossil fuel-dependent vision of energy security, endorsed by mainstream trade unions in the name of 'jobs'. Labour's vision for Brexit needs to put forward a fundamentally class, community and climate change-based approach that moves away from airport expansion, fracking and fossil fuels.

BREXIT AS CONFLICT

The media-backed rightwing Brexit camp stoked the marginalisation of a 'British public', a singular identity of British-born and majority white Christian citizens – who had been marginalised by the unaccountable bureaucrats of the EU, who had undermined a sovereign population's ability to make its own decisions. The enemy was Brussels and immigrants, refugees, sliding to general 'outsiders' – Muslim and black and brown communities – competing for scarce resources – jobs, housing, health care, and welfare. 'Taking back control' would be empowering, the box to tick to shake the establishment, although in reality the establishment was holding both boxes.

Racism, class, poverty and capitalism were marginalised by this discourse. It was a nationalistic narrative promoted by corporate and establishment interests seeking to maintain a system based on a continuing subordination and marginalisation of working class people wherever they come from.

The leftist Lexit camp mobilised through the trope of the organised, diverse British working class, with shared interests and history, driving towards a planned, socialist economy. Control 'over the supply of labour' was to be a key part of this, and neoliberal trade deals and directives such as the Posted Workers Directive were to be scrapped. The PWD allows companies to employ overseas workers at different rates of pay but not less than the minimum wage in host countries, enabling them to work where wages are higher, but contributing to a divided, multiple-tiered workforce undermining the rights of all workers in the workplace and their capacity to collectively bargain.

The Lexit camp characterised the EU as a capitalist club designed to enforce wage restraint, undermine trade unions and prevent the British working class from realising the power to win.[3] Controlling the supply of labour would be necessary to do this. The working class in this conception were framed as British citizens. The marginalised left-wing British working class would need to marginalise the migrant working class in order to achieve its aims.

The mainstream Remain camp narrative matched the political representation of the EU by the EU – a community of nations, co-operation and mutual aid. Advocates by turns invoked inter-state solidarity and the benefits of freedom of movement for all *citizens*. Immigrants were 'a benefit' to the economy, mass net contributors, entrepreneurs. The responsibility of the EU in maintaining a disempowered working class, whose freedoms amounted to choosing which country to be exploited in, went unaddressed.

The existence of trade deals which sell off public services and assets and the dominant neoliberal economic framework within which 'development' would evolve were also unmentioned. The complicity of EU states in permitting the blocking, drowning and incarceration of refugees in camps, rather than allowing them access to the resources and rights that citizens have, helped marginalise migrant, British and non-British working class experiences of exploitation and exclusion.

The leftwing Remain camp, which included Greece's former Minister of Finance Yanis Varoufakis, comprised those who saw the choice as a 'lose-lose' one. The benefits of being able to move in search of better conditions and work, gaining protection from some of the rulings which have enabled equal pay and a limit to working hours, were seen as a restraint on employer abuses.[4]

This position was a defensive one, against the prospect of being at the mercy of a more nationalist British establishment which could take back even more control over working conditions, borders, trade unions, the public sector and trade. This compromise marginalised the potential for breaking up a powerful neoliberal institution, whose existence is actually a driver of the marginalising processes which are being opposed, leading Lexit critics to label Left Remainers as nonsensical and unambitious.

These very general descriptions of the way the Brexit debate was framed will in their brevity sideline other positions, but they demonstrate some of the conflicts within attitudes towards Brexit.

WHOSE BREXIT?

Understanding more about who voted, how and why is critical. Whilst it hasn't been possible to quantify the motivations of any group of voters fully, the June 2017 British Social Attitudes Survey, based on interviewing 3,000 people, found nearly three-quarters of those who are "worried about immigration" voted Leave, compared with 36% who did not identify this as a concern.[5]

The Leave – Remain divide has been quantified in race, class, age, education and economic income terms, yet the statistics do not cover the *experience* of those who voted. Leave voters came from areas with the lowest wages in the country and where there was a high proportion of unskilled jobs.[6] Remain areas specialised in jobs with higher pay. According to analysts EMSI, Leave areas have their highest specialisations in industrial jobs, ranging from tool-makers to production line workers; Remain areas have their highest specialisations in creative and professional roles, with arts, advertising and journalism riding high.[7] These are jobs where workers have a high degree of control over their own labour and working day.

Two-thirds of those describing themselves as Asian voted Remain, as did 73% of black voters, whilst nearly six in ten of those describing themselves as Christian voted Leave; seven in ten voting Muslims voted to Remain.[8] These figures don't reveal the conditions working class people of colour experience, with Bangladeshi household incomes £8,900 a year (35%) lower than the white British median and typical black households £5,600 less (22%). These income gaps widen after housing costs are accounted for, given that 58% of white British families own their own home, while only one in four Bangladeshi, black and other white (primarily European) families do.[9]

LSE research concluded that a greater pool of migrant labour for employers to exploit does not drive down wages. Pay did fall by 0.7% in some areas, which is not insignificant if you are on a minimal income.[10] It also did not appear to take into account the impact of reduced overtime and hours and intensification of the labour process, or the fact that the floor of wage rights – the minimum wage – is actually a ceiling in many workplaces. This suggests that while a greater pool of workers for managers to choose from may not drive down wages, *unorganised* workers can be used to *keep wages low* by undermining collective bargaining in the absence of unionisation drives.[11]

The current legislative and contractual framework in which work is organised is more significant in undermining the rights of migrant workers than their origins or language barriers. A recent cleaners' strike saw agency workers sourced from Norwich and Scotland undermine striking Serco cleaners, showing that workers need not be sourced from overseas to undermine collective bargaining, given the flexibility of contracts and relative impunity of employers.[12]

LABOUR IS PEOPLE

Contrary to the Lexit and Labour argument that constricting the supply of labour is the answer to a lack of organisation in the workplace, a massive investment in organising migrant workers and cracking down on modern slavery from a worker-centred perspective is required. Trade union rhetoric and intention is not matched by the funding and focus needed to do this. Funding education, training and organisers who speak the language of workers from countries of high migration is key, not just to union renewal, but to social change in the UK.

An example: the hospitality industry is the fourth biggest employer in the UK.[13] It has one of the highest proportions of migrant and BME workers (70%) and the lowest union density in the country – 3.6%[14] and some of the highest incidences of exploitation and discrimination.[15] The biggest trade union in the country – Unite – of which I am a member and for whom I worked since 2005 for seven years, has just two full-time organisers in this sector. The London hotel workers branch runs on a shoestring and uses volunteer translators. The helpline for Unite members does not offer advice in languages other than English. We can't organise complex workplaces on the cheap. The mainstream trade unions are yet to meet the challenge of organising in the most casualised sectors, even if the smaller, more agile, non-bureaucratic unions such as United Voices of the World and the Industrial Workers of Great Britain can.

The idea of workplaces with union recognition agreements being the only ones to permit migrant labour – an idea put forward by the Unite General Secretary Len McCluskey[16] and potentially on the table for Labour – should not be confused with union strength and the closed shop. The imposition of these conditions by law risks barring workers from industries and pushing people into undocumented work. To implement union labour only workplaces would need massive enforcement given that workplaces employing migrant labour are not only big agricultural, logistics and processing factories and warehouses, but also small firms, restaurants and hotels. An extension of the minimum wage inspectorate and the Gangmasters and Labour Abuse Authority which is currently playing a policing role in enforcing the 'hostile environment' directive would be needed. This approach is not a trade union or worker-led led one to organisation, but one of state enforcement, which could actually result in trade unions playing the role of border guard, restricting access to jobs for fellow workers by visa status and nationality.

BREXIT MEANS NEW BORDERS

Already Human Resource Management analysts and corporate lawyers predict a lobbied-for modification of TUPE (Transfer of

Undertakings (Protection of Employment)) legislation to allow for 'harmonisation' of terms and conditions between workers transferring from one employer to another. This is expected to follow a wage suppression trend.[17] Others are arguing that TUPE should not apply to Small and Medium Enterprises. These can easily be created through the current lax agency laws which allow companies to fold and resurface with the same staff, offices and directors but without liabilities for the workers they just decided not to pay, leading to even fewer rights for agency workers.

UK case law, such as the recent victories by Unison on scrapping tribunal fees and the right for workers in union-recognised workplaces to be consulted over contractual changes, is not expected to be impacted but caps in equality case compensation, and changes to sick pay and holiday rights are being lobbied for.[18]

Labour's proposed repeal of the dozen or more Conservative legal instruments designed to restrict and criminalise trade union activity also needs to be accompanied by a trade union education programme delivered through schools, colleges, Labour and Momentum media and trade unions to encourage and normalise union organising as common sense. Sanctions against employers – currently, largely only subjected to fines and compensation awards – who violate workers' rights need to be substantial enough to act as a deterrent to current practices of victimise first, pay later. Focusing on restricting freedom of movement, rather than employer impunity, marginalises the responsibility of businesses which treat all workers as expendable.

TAKING BACK CONTROL

Capital is attempting to colonise resources for social reproduction by restricting migrants' access to services before coming for 'us'. The Immigration Act creates conditions for future privatisation of not only our public services, but public life and rights to a commons.[19]

Landlords are demanding passport checks in order to rent property.[20] Property, even temporary, is defined by the Government as a prerequisite for accessing treaty rights (right to residency) – currently rough-sleeping EU nationals are being seized from the streets by Immigration Enforcement Teams (with the help of charities), locked in detention centres and deported.[21] This process is facing judicial review, thanks to activists and pro-bono lawyers with North East London Migrant Action.[22] The Department for Education's gathering of nationality and birthplace data in the school census is to be shared with the Home Office in order to target families for deportation, effectively making the right to free education conditional on status.[23] Access to free health care has been axed for migrants – with proof of identity increasingly sought by medics. Now both a private insurance and payment system has been established which can be extended to citizens in future.[24] Racial profiling is an inherent part of this process leading to an escalation of racist othering in schools, clinics, by landlords, the mainstream media and on the streets.

PAPERS, VISA, UNION CARD, PLEASE

At the last count, the UK had 34 different types of visa in operation.[25] Even if you are an 'exceptional talent' in science, humanities, etc., and wish to realise your potential in the UK, you need exceptionally large sums of cash. The application will cost you £292, unrefundable if rejected, and a further £293 if accepted.

'Barista Visas' (based on current two year Youth Mobility Visas), 'London Visas' (for Square Mile financial sector employees), 'Brickie Visas' (a three year points-based visa), and seasonal, sectoral, regional (Australia and Canada have them), age and occupational points-based schemes have all been suggested as methods of managing migration by the Government's Migrant Advisory Committee. Access to any state welfare support will be axed. Replacing migrant workers with machines has also been suggested as an alternative to plugging the skills gap.[26]

New visas, statuses and forms of sponsorship will create new markets of labour purchase for employers – possibly jointly brokered by trade unions – and new markets for visa trading, people trafficking and further exploitation of undocumented workers. During the passage of the Modern Slavery Act, the Government slashed the rights of victims to recover unpaid wages to just two years. According to the Anti-Trafficking and Labour Exploitation

Unit, if the UK leaves the EU it will be far more difficult to challenge this restriction and if the Human Rights Act is scrapped, it may be impossible.[27]

Germany, and Denmark with the agreement of Danish trade unions, have applied differential status for refugees within the labour market and lower wages – one euro per hour in the case of one German work programme[28] – in workfare-style bonded apprenticeships, tying workers to employer-registered accommodation and sponsorship.[29] Devaluing the price of labour undermines the rights of people seeking refuge and collective strength and bargaining. Labour's 'managed migration' should not follow this divisive route

Restricting access to healthcare, education, welfare, work, equal rights, property and representation for millions of people living in the UK signals a new round of marginalisation, and an intensification of the class system, leading to a form of social death for non-citizens.

MARGINS BURN

The devaluation of black lives in the UK to the point that they are expendable and the continuing denial of this crisis[30] correspond with an ongoing colonial process by capital of resource extraction and accumulation which deny life and designate entire habitats as sacrifice zones.[31,32] These can be regions in the global south or they can be in the UK, including in the most unequal and expensive borough in the capital – the Royal Borough of Kensington and Chelsea.[33]

What has the Grenfell catastrophe to do with Brexit? It represents the consequence of multiple marginalisations – by those with drastically more power and privilege, wealth, whiteness, qualifications, confidence and freedom of movement, possessed by council leaders, decision-makers, developers, landlords, employers, media commentators, the newspaper editors who sanctioned ridicule and smear stories – marginalising the economic and social factors which led to the catastrophe – all pushing millions of people to the margins, which in the case of Grenfell Tower, led to their deaths.[34]

THE MAINSTREAM MEDIA AS A MARGINALISATION MACHINE

Researching this chapter, I kept noticing how online searches consistently reproduced the voices of those who were already empowered. The representational universe on Brexit is highly mediated.

Momentum-related activists put on a series of events in split Leave and Remain cities under the banner of 'Take Back Control' to bring together Leave and Remain voters and try to process some of the dynamics which informed people's fears and desires.[35] Whilst they tended to attract mostly politicised left-wing Remain voters, the events, with their conflict-welcoming opening sessions, were still a model for engaging people from across the vote divide.

Momentum organised dozens of Bernie Sanders' Get Out The Vote campaign-inspired training sessions in doorstep election canvassing. These enabled a break with mediated communication into mass face-to-face outreach. Hundreds queued on Friday evenings in central London to train and thousands took part in nationwide sessions, basically on how to speak to each other.[36] This helped transform the election campaign in its directness, unpredictability and de-centering of already privileged opinions and voices.

A similar process should explore some of the drivers of the Brexit vote – Leave or Remain and the changes that are trying to emerge through it. Conversations, not mediated by commentators with massive media platforms, are going to be experienced face-to-face. A deep democratic understanding of the ways we have come to marginalise and be marginalised, within our relationships, our workplaces, our communities and ourselves needs to happen.

The role of Labour and Momentum activists and leaders should be to develop the Labour manifesto as a guide for a participatory Brexit policy, explored through *conflict facilitation* across the country, fostering well-facilitated meetings where conflict is not suppressed or 'resolved' but processed, and where marginalising power is named and understood.

Brexit is a conflict of marginalisations, deliberately polarised by the yes-no question and the framing of the idea of 'taking our country back' by powerful elites. Negotiations which "seek to unite the country around a Brexit deal that works for every community in Britain" need to involve everyone. Despite its current elite unaccountability, Brexit can be reclaimed at a grassroots level, as an entrance into a new political understanding, process and polity.

3. TOWARDS A NATIONAL EDUCATION SERVICE

Kiri Tunks

MANIFESTO SUMMARY

Everyone should have the opportunity to access education throughout their lives. To meet this responsibility, Labour will create a National Education Service for England to provide life-long learning free at the point of use.

A Labour Government will overhaul existing childcare arrangements to create high-quality childcare places in mixed environments with direct government subsidy, so that everyone has access to affordable childcare. We will transition to a qualified, graduate-led workforce and extend the 30 free hours of childcare to all two-year-olds. We will halt the closure of Sure Start centres and increase the programme's funding.

On schools, Labour will not waste money on free schools or grammars. A fairer funding formula will be introduced, standards will be improved and democratic accountability strengthened to ensure schools serve the public interest and local communities. We will also invest in measures to close the attainment gap between children from different backgrounds. We will reduce class sizes to less than 30 for all five to seven year olds, introduce free school meals for all primary school children and establish a commission to look into curriculum and assessment. Ending the public sector cap and a national pay settlement will help improve teacher recruitment and retention, as will tackling teacher workloads. Schools-based counselling will be extended to all schools, as well as an inclusive strategy for children with special educational needs.

Labour will introduce free education in further education colleges, which will benefit from new investment and have a target for all teaching staff to have a teaching qualification within five years. The Educational Maintenance Allowance for 16 to 18 year olds, scrapped by the Conservatives, will be reintroduced.

On apprenticeships, Labour will take steps to ensure that both high quality is maintained and the quantity increased. Trade union representation in the governance structures of the Institute of Apprenticeships will be guaranteed and targets set to increase the number of apprenticeships for people with disabilities. For university students, tuition fees will be scrapped and maintenance grants reintroduced.

***

Education is what empowers us all to realise our full potential but in Britain the system is in crisis. The dream we had of a fully integrated comprehensive education system, free at the point of use, with highly qualified and resourceful staff able to deliver an inspirational, challenging and enjoyable education is in tatters. The education system is increasingly atomised, distorted by a premise of choice for parents and students when the truth is that public money is being squandered on the entrepreneurial experimentations of free schools and academies. The central role of the local authority has largely disappeared with those maintained schools that are left now scrabbling around to find the specialist services they need.

Education is big business – globally it is estimated to be worth £4 trillion. But its value is actually beyond measure to the millions who look to it to transform lives – improving life chances of individuals and the collective well-being of all of us in society.

Successive governments have lost sight of this mission. Education is now run almost entirely without consideration for a child's needs beyond what is required to get them to hit a dubious target, often set for them early in primary school. We are operating in a high-stakes testing regime which is generating horrendous levels of workload and stress for both children and staff.

Labour's manifesto was therefore something of a lifebelt to those who work in education who are struggling to stay afloat, to retain something of what brought us into teaching. It offered hope that, in government, Labour could provide an alternative to the current marketised, privatised and test-focused education system that exploits teachers and reduces children to raw scores. It didn't offer everything we may want but it went a long way to setting out an alternative vision for education that puts children's interests first. But to achieve its alternative, Labour has some enormous challenges to overcome, brought about since 2010 with the start of the Conservatives' neoliberal reforms in education.

RECRUITMENT AND RETENTION

The first of these is the crisis in teacher recruitment and retention. In October 2016, the Government confirmed that nearly a third of teachers who joined the profession in 2010 had left teaching within their first five years: of the 21,400 teachers who started working in English state schools in 2010, over 6,400 (30%) had quit by 2015.[1] Department for Education (DfE) figures show that this trend is continuing: of the teachers who joined the profession in 2011, only 69% were still teaching five years later. A young teacher in my school who qualified two years ago is the only one out of a group of five friends who is still teaching. DfE figures for 2016 reveal that more than 100,000 potential teachers have never taught, despite finishing their training.[2] What Labour does next could act as a ladder to help this pool of inactive teachers rejoin the profession.

Why are so many teachers leaving, despite committing to a postgraduate qualification? A survey published in October 2015 by the NUT and YouGov found that over half of teachers who were thinking of leaving teaching in the next two years cited "volume of workload" (61%) and "seeking better work/life balance" (57%) as the two top issues causing them to consider this.[3] This is disastrous at a time when pupil numbers are rising sharply. In July 2017, the DfE reported that the number of children enrolled in state schools would increase by almost 800,000 within the next decade.[4] The Institute for Fiscal Studies (IFS) estimates that, in order to maintain the current pupil-teacher ratio, there would need to be an additional 30,000 teachers in the profession by 2020 to deal with the increase in pupil numbers.[5]

We are also seeing an increase of unqualified teachers or teachers teaching outside their specialisms. For example, in 2016 only 63% of physics and 75% of chemistry teachers held a relevant post A-level qualification in the subject. For maths and English, these figures were 78% and 81% respectively.[6] In November 2016, there were 500 fewer qualified teachers in service than in the previous year. Conversely, there were 1,400 more teachers in-service without qualified teacher status than there had been the year before.[7] Labour's own survey has revealed that more than 600,000 pupils in England are now taught by unqualified teachers.[8]

Then there is teacher pay. We are now subject to an unfair Performance-Related Pay (PRP) system that works within the further restraints of the School Teachers Review Body (STRB). Despite the STRB recommending last year that teachers needed a significant uplift, once again teachers face a below inflation pay rise. Since 2010, teachers have suffered a real-term pay-cut of 15%.[9] Furthermore, the system of awarding pay on progression towards set targets has resulted in real inequalities. A survey carried out by the NUT of nearly 5,000 members showed that half of all teachers felt their school's pay policy was unfair and 60% said that PRP has undermined appraisal for professional development purposes.[10] In particular, Black and Asian teachers are more likely to be denied progression than white British teachers; part-time teachers are almost twice as likely to be denied progression as full-time teachers; and progression rates are far lower in primary schools than in secondary schools.

Labour's plans to end the public-sector pay cap and reintroduce the Schools Support Staff Negotiating Body and national pay settlements for teachers are welcome. However, it will need to be supported by the necessary funds to make fair pay achievable.

FUNDING CUTS

Alongside the teacher recruitment and retention crisis, schools and colleges are facing huge funding cuts. The impact of the Government's unfair funding plans was apparent to many in the election and helps explain why education became such a priority issue for voters.

Another vote winner for Labour was the pledge to end tuition fees and restore maintenance grants. University should not be something our young people rule out for fear of debt. We would also like to see a commitment to restoring the Educational Maintenance Grant for FE students which previously supported so many young people to continue into Further Education.

The Education Services Grant, which funds spending on school improvement, management of school buildings and tackling non-attendance, was cut by £200 million (around 20%) in 2015-16. Even larger cuts are planned in the next few years, which will mean the loss of a wide range of services provided for schools by local authorities such as school improvement, behavioural and pupil support services, music services and outdoor education as well as libraries, youth services and child protection support.

The NUT's School Cuts website presented figures from the government and the Institute for Fiscal Studies which clearly laid out the impact of all the cuts for each individual school in the country.[11] Voters could see for themselves how Conservative spin was hiding the truth about school funding. It was apparent to all that Labour's manifesto offered the best hope for schools everywhere and caused 750,000 voters to change their vote.[12]

Labour's commitment to invest in education, by reversing the Conservatives' cuts, promising that schools will have the resources they need, and that no school would lose out through a new funding formula, was music to the ears of both educational professionals and parents. Likewise the Party's commitment to invest in new school buildings, including the phased removal of asbestos from existing schools, signalled that the party had a long-term vision for, and commitment to, state education. Equally welcome was Labour's pledge to stop wasting money on "inefficient free schools and the Conservatives' grammar schools". This recognised that they are a dangerous vanity project aimed at privatising our education system. At the moment, the only new schools that are allowed to open are free schools. Forty-two free schools have opened in areas with no predicted need for additional places, at a cost of at least £241 million and local authorities are unable to plan to meet community needs.[13] There is no evidence that free schools, or academies, have any better impact on the standards in our schools but each costs on average 33% more than a local authority primary school and 51% more for a secondary.[14] The National Audit Office (NAO) has also highlighted the huge waste of money spent on land acquisitions for free schools, with purchasers often paying above the market price.[15] Meanwhile, maintained schools are not receiving the investment that they need. Capital spending on schools and colleges has been cut by over one-third in re-al-terms since 2010-11. The NAO report stated that it would cost some £6.7 billion to repair all school buildings to a satis-factory standard.[16]

LOCAL ACCOUNTABILITY

Labour's commitment to ensure that all schools will be demo-cratically accountable and serve the public interest and local communities is a vital change. The NUT believes that publicly funded state schools should come back under local authority controls, but in the meantime, local authorities must be given the power and the funding to open new schools where necessary. Crucially, support for students with special educational needs has been, or is likely to be, reduced. Many schools across the country already say they have insufficient funding to adequately provide for these pupils.

Government cuts to local authority funding mean a significant reduction in the support available to schools, while the changes to the high needs funding system do not take account of the value that local authority support can add. Local authority cuts are also putting extra strain on home to school transport for disabled children.

We know that given the time and the resources, teachers can work brilliantly in collaborative and supportive ways to improve the life chances of young people. But any government serious about making this possible must look at workload. Teachers are routinely working over 55 hours a week, much of it spent on tasks that do not benefit students. One example is widespread expectation that primary teachers take photographs of practical work to prove the work was done. This kind of excessive accountability and an obsession with a high-stakes testing regime are turning our schools into "exam factories", as referenced by ex-teacher and NUT member and newly elected MP for Hull West & Hessle, Emma Hardy, in her maiden speech.[17]

A future Labour government must address these problems at their root otherwise nothing will change except, perhaps, the numbers of teachers leaving. Labour's manifesto said: "We trust in teachers and support staff professionalism to refocus their workload on what happens in the classroom." This move would be universally welcomed.

THE QUALITY OF EDUCATION

Labour's pledge to reduce class sizes to less than 30 for all five to seven year olds is a good start but no child of any age should be in a class of more than 30. A country serious about equalising chances for all its children should be aiming for class sizes of 20 across all phases.

All children are suffering from a narrowing of the curriculum and less flexibility in teaching styles. Primary schools are under the yoke of SATs targets; for secondary schools it is the ever-changing targets of 5 A* to C GCSEs, now Progress 8, or is it Ebacc? Both are new performance indicators introduced by the Conservative Government. And as the levels keep changing so floor targets do too. Teachers are trying to stay steady on a vessel that is increasingly unstable. This creates a very stressful environment for teaching and learning.

Many primary students face a sparse diet of literacy and numeracy with a sprinkling of other subjects. Secondary students are expected to specialise much earlier with many picking GCSEs in Year 8 from an ever-decreasing set of options. Subjects like art, music, drama and Design & Technology are all losing curriculum time. Some students are pushed into subjects they don't like just so the school can hit an EBacc target.

A study carried out by the National Union of Teachers/Association of Teachers & Lecturers with over 1,000 parents and staff in 2015 raised serious concerns about the efficacy and benefits of baseline assessment. Dr Alice Bradbury, UCL Institute of Education, said:

> The study found that baseline assessment is seen by teachers as ineffective and potentially damaging because it is time-consuming, distracts from the important settling in period in reception and does not provide any additional useful information. There are serious doubts about the accuracy of baseline as an assessment, particularly given the age of the children, and as a result there are real questions over its value in education.[18]

These criticisms can equally be applied to the notorious SATs tests which have been subject to widespread calls for a parental and teaching boycott. Apart from the stress of the exams themselves, it is the impact on the whole school experience which concerns many of us. The curriculum is largely planned to fit the needs of SATs, resulting in a narrow diet of learning for many young people and skewing the focus of their education to a reductive target. There are serious questions about the benefit of what is being tested (students' use of fronted adverbials, for example) and the reliability of marking and administration which has damaged the reputation of such tests.

Research carried out for the NUT by Professor Merryn Hutchins and published as *Exam Factories?* showed that:

- Test scores have increased but this is not necessarily reflective of children's level of understanding, knowledge and skills.

- Teaching is heavily focused on material that will be tested – other areas of the curriculum, such as the arts, humanities and sciences are being squeezed out.
- Some children come to believe at a very young age that they have 'failed'. This results in low self-esteem and disaffection.
- There is an increase in stress, anxiety and mental health problems among children and young people linked to school work or exams.
- The young people who suffer most are those who are from disadvantaged backgrounds and/or who have special education needs.[19]

We are not preparing our children for the 21st century or a globalised world. This obsession with teaching only what can be measured means we are denying our young people vital skills they will need. Personal, Social & Health Education and citizenship are forgotten subjects in many schools. Along with a reduction of pastoral time, this means there is little space for free discussion or exploration of current affairs. Instead we have the Prevent programme which is meant to stop young people from becoming radicalised but which, in many places, has done more to demonise and alienate them than engage with them. Meanwhile, significant numbers of our young people are being groomed in other ways, by gangs, drugs and child sexual exploitation. Where is the curriculum time to address these things?

Labour's commitment to abandon plans to reintroduce baseline assessments and launch a commission to look into curriculum and assessment, starting by reviewing Key Stage 1 and 2 SATs is very welcome and is what the NUT has been calling for. We know that the world's most successful education systems use more continuous assessment, which avoids 'teaching for the test' and frees the curriculum so it can meet the needs of the child. The pressure on schools to hit targets and keep the OFSTED inspector wolf from the door means we are losing sight of the well-being of the child, with increasing levels of diagnosed mental health conditions. ChildLine, the counselling service for children and young people, has reported that school and exam pressures were one of the biggest causes of feelings of stress and anxiety among children and young people. There has been a 200% increase in all age groups in counselling sessions related to school and education problems, particularly in relation to exams.[20]

In both 2007 and 2011, a UNICEF study of the well-being of children in England showed that England compared poorly to other OECD countries for child well-being.[21]

The well-being of children should be higher on the agenda of all policymakers, so Labour's plans to extend schools-based counselling to all schools to improve children's mental health are good news. But it must be properly funded and school staff must receive both the time and the training to implement it properly. We also believe that Government must address the causes of the stress rather than deal solely with the symptoms. We need a serious review of our curriculum and the punitive testing regime to ensure that our school system works for our children and not just for OFSTED data collection.

All children should have access to high-quality pre-school care which should be staffed by well-paid, well-trained professionals. Increasingly, the Early Years and Primary phases are becoming another part of the education production line, getting children 'school-ready', when they should be focusing on child-centred play and learning. Labour's commitment to Sure Start, high quality Early Years education and universal joined-up services is a sign of a policy which is grounded in evidence and experience. But the Party must engage with the urgent issue of the number of nursery schools and children's centres closing up across the country due to increased costs and less funding.

CONCLUSION

Given the onslaught of criticisms and attacks faced by teachers over the last few years, it's a wonder we have any teachers left. Despite the high attrition rate of teachers nationally, huge numbers are still attracted to the profession and want to stay – for the children. If Labour truly wants to improve education, it needs to respect and listen to the knowledge and judgement of the professionals, ensure education is centred on the needs of the learner and commit the funding necessary to resource the high-quality education system our young people deserve. The NUT looks forward to working with Labour to turn its aspirations for the education system into reality.

4. A FAIR DEAL AT WORK

Gregor Gall

MANIFESTO SUMMARY

A Labour Government will invest in a new Ministry of Labour that will give new powers to workers and their trade unions, reviewing the rules on union recognition and strengthening workplace rights. Specifically, we will introduce a 20-point plan for security and equality at work, including equal rights from the first day of employment, a ban on zero hours contracts, the repeal of the Trade Union Act, four new public holidays, raising the Minimum Wage to the level of the Living Wage, a maximum pay ratio, a ban on unpaid internships, the abolition of employment tribunal fees and a public enquiry into blacklisting. Additionally, a future Labour Government will scrap recent Conservative legislation that weakened the rights of contract workers and initiate consultations on the introduction of statutory bereavement leave and legislation to permit secure online workplace balloting.

On self-employed workers, Labour will clamp down on bogus self-employment, which is imposed on workers by unscrupulous employers to avoid costs and their duties to workers. We will also extend the rights of employees to all workers, substantially improving the quality of life for those in insecure work. We will also establish a commission to modernise the law around employment status.

***

Labour's section of its 2017 general election manifesto on matters of work and employment was called 'A Fair Deal at Work'. Fairness is now quite a ubiquitous but also vague term. It can mean and represent many different things to many different people and groups. One merely has to recall 'New' Labour's 1998 'Fairness at Work' White Paper, which became the Employment Relations Act 1999, to understand that fairness is an ambiguous and often contested concept and is subject to political pressures based upon class alignments. In the case of the Employment Relations Act 1999, the Conservatives' anti-union laws of the 1980s and 1990s were not repealed; the means for gaining statutory union recognition were made 'business-friendly' after lobbying from employers; and employers, through the CBI, were then directly given the right to influence the Act's provisions, especially on the crucial topic of union recognition. Tony Blair boasted in the aforementioned 'Fairness at Work' White Paper that, despite the forthcoming changes in the Employment Relations Act 1999, Britain would still have "the most lightly regulated labour market of any leading economy in the world". In other words, the changes would be little and light, so that employers would still be able to enforce their desired forms of flexibility on pay, working hours and so on.

In stark contrast, there was little room left for ambiguity on the issues of work and employment in the manifesto upon which the Corbyn-led Labour Party fought the 2017 general election. It was about representing and advancing the interests of the many workers – and not the few – employers and managers. It was not only a step change from the 'New' Labour years but also a big advance from the Labour Party under Ed Miliband and the 2015 general election manifesto. This chapter begins by outlining the key components of the 2017 manifesto in order to carry out the task of deepening and extending them for a future general election.

MANIFESTO COMMITMENTS

The opening sentence of the section of the Labour manifesto on work and employment could have come from any political party, promising 'motherhood and apple pie', namely, "Work should provide people with security and fulfilment. But for too many people work is insecure and does not make ends meet". Yet it was what came next that distinguished the Labour manifesto from all other political parties' manifestos. This was the twenty point plan for "security and equality at work":

- equal rights from day one, whether workers are part-time or full-time, temporary or permanent
- ban zero hours contracts
- ensure any employer wishing to recruit labour from abroad does not undercut workers at home

- repeal the Trade Union Act and roll out sectoral collective bargaining
- guarantee trade unions a right to access workplaces
- four new public holidays
- raise the minimum wage to the level of the independent living wage
- end the public sector pay cap
- amend the takeover code to ensure every takeover proposal has a clear plan in place to protect workers and pensioners
- maximum pay ratios of 20:1 in the public sector and in companies bidding for public contracts
- ban unpaid internships
- enforce all workers' rights to union representation at work
- abolish employment tribunal fees
- double paid paternity leave to four weeks and increase paternity pay
- strengthen protections for women against unfair redundancy on grounds of pregnancy
- hold a public enquiry into blacklisting
- give equalities reps statutory rights
- reinstate protection against third party harassment
- use public spending power to drive up standards
- introduce a civil enforcement system to ensure compliance with gender pay auditing

In addition to these headline pledges, the manifesto also committed to providing standard employment contracts for part-time workers; reversing the recent weakening of Transfer of Undertakings (Protection of Employment) regulations; abolishing the loophole on agency workers regulations known as the 'Swedish derogation'; introducing statutory bereavement leave, for time off work after the loss of close family members; toughening the law against assaulting workers who have to enforce new regulations; permitting secure online and workplace balloting for industrial action votes and internal union elections; and strengthening redundancy arrangements to bring workers in Britain more into line with their European counterparts. On self-employment in the 'gig economy', construction and elsewhere, the manifesto promised to clamp down on bogus self-employment by (i) shifting the burden of proof, so that the law assumes a worker is an employee unless the employer can prove otherwise; (ii) banning 'umbrella' companies; (iii) imposing punitive fines on employers not meeting their responsibilities, helping to deter others from doing the same; and (iv) establishing a commission to modernise the law around employment status.

The manifesto also provided a short rationale for making each of these pledges. These were based around making work pay, in terms of pay rates and hours made available, making work secure and establishing equal rights for workers, as well as facilitating the means by which the collective organs of representation of workers, namely, unions, could also help achieve these outcomes. These commitments were based upon

(i) recognising that the state needs to intervene in labour market processes to ensure fairer outcomes, given that voluntary means provide no compulsion to change employers' behaviour; (ii) re-instating the notion of the state as a model employer especially in the public sector and in public procurement; (iii) understanding the need to end the race to the bottom by stopping undercutting of wages and conditions by creating a legally enforceable floor of rights on terms and conditions of employment. Labour also committed itself in government to ensure Britain abides by the global labour standards of the International Labour Organisation conventions. Moreover, the manifesto in the section on work and employment – as well as elsewhere in its 100-plus pages – also understood that decent pay and conditions along with secure employment had to be situated in the context of stable economic growth where the fruits of that growth are more evenly distributed. Consequently, manifesto commitments on investment in public infrastructure, returning privatised utilities and services to the public sector, and progressive taxation policies were necessarily part of the vision on work and employment.

Some further observations are pertinent here so that the degree of innovation, radicalism and progress can be fully appreciated. It was a bold move to state that sectoral collective bargaining will be implemented, as it was to say a maximum pay ratio would be introduced. Similarly, pledging to create a new Ministry of Labour, with union representation on its executive board and providing the resources for adequate enforcement was audacious. Some pledges necessarily reprise earlier attempts at change like Paul Farrelly's Temporary and Agency Workers (Prevention of Less Favourable Treatment) Bill of 2007. However, and whilst acknowledging that even the longest manifestos are routinely short on detail, it is still salient to observe that many of the pledges require considerable thought about how they will be implemented in order to ensure the desired outcomes are achieved. For example, forcing unwilling employers in any one individual sector of the economy to bargain together will take tough measures as many do not want to bargain with unions and do not want to do so alongside their fellow competitors. Similarly, strengthening the statutory process by which unions can gain union recognition will require that an offence of unfair labour practices, like stopping employers from threatening redundancies or divestment, be created.

There were also some obvious gaps in the pledges. Amongst them are health and safety, like increasing the Health and Safety Executive's power and resources so that workplaces are routinely visited, assessed and modified where necessary; industrial democracy, like establishing worker directors and enhancing the power of statutory works councils; taking the opportunity of repealing the Trade Union Act 2016 with a positive menu of rights, especially on industrial action, for unions; and enforcing gender pay equality, rather than just compelling employers to publish data on the extent of the gender pay inequality.

So to this extent, the manifesto pledges on work and employment were not the 'finished article' and should be seen more as a work-in-progress, where the option exists to deepen and extend the direction of travel that has already been laid out by the manifesto. Indeed, the snap nature of the election meant that the normal process for determining the content of the manifesto could not be undertaken. This also meant that the Workforce 2020 consultation exercise with affiliates, constituency parties and interested parties could not be concluded, nor could the fruits it has furnished so far be used. In this context, this chapter returns to two prior documents to help the process of deepening and extending the manifesto pledges on work and employment. The first is the Institute of Employment Rights' *A Manifesto for Labour Law* and the second is John McDonnell's private members' bill, the Trade Union Freedom Bill.

A MANIFESTO FOR LABOUR LAW

In June 2016, the Institute of Employment Rights[1] launched its *A Manifesto for Labour Law* (Ewing et al. 2016) at Westminster with Shadow Chancellor, John McDonnell MP, and Shadow Minister for Trade Unions, Ian Lavery MP, alongside leaders from several major unions. The 25 policy recommendations were warmly received that day and since then almost all unions have supported them. Then, in September 2016, John McDonnell, at Labour Party Conference, announced that the next Labour government would look to implement the IER's policies. The *Manifesto* fed into the Labour Party's Workforce 2020 consultation where the hope was that it would be adopted and implemented in full by a future Labour government. To help in this process, the *Manifesto* was condensed down into 'A Twelve Point Plan for Labour' to build upon it, which included proposals for worker representation on company boards and works councils with binding rights. This turn of event, while to be heartily welcomed, was not altogether surprising for the proposals in *A Manifesto for Labour Law* were developed at the request of Jeremy Corbyn's team in its determination to advance workers' rights.

The premise of *A Manifesto for Labour Law* is to shift the focus of labour law from statutory minimum rights to collective bargaining, allowing workers to organise and negotiate for higher wages and conditions within not only their companies but across entire sectors. Such sectoral collective bargaining could lead to wage and condition floors being set across industries, which can be built on at company level. This should lead to higher pay and better conditions, adding to workers' job security and income. This strategy amounts to using the law as an enabler rather than being wholly reliant upon it to deliver protection, whilst recognising that without strong unions, individual employment rights are too difficult to enforce at a workplace level. Moreover, it also recognises that too strong a focus on individual employment rights wrongly suggests that the only role of the state is to enforce minimum standards with everything else left to determination by the market.

However, *A Manifesto for Labour Law* also recommends that the definition of the legal term 'worker' is reviewed so that all workers are covered, notwithstanding the attempts to impose the bogus status of 'self-employed' upon them. The repercussions for those employers who break the rules are both punitive and deterrent in nature. Part of this would involve rebuilding the regime of regulation and enforcement through having labour inspectors within workplaces to make sure the law is followed, labour courts specifically focused on employment cases, and sanctioning unscrupulous employers including through criminal proceedings.

Sectoral (industry-wide, multi-employer) collective bargaining along the lines deployed in Germany, Sweden, Norway and Denmark works by creating a floor of collectively bargained basic terms applicable to all employers in the sector. The terms are binding on all employers within the sector, whether or not they recognise unions or participate in the bargaining process. The minimum terms can be improved upon through local bargaining or in individual employment contracts, but they cannot be undercut. This forces employers to compete with each other by innovating and investing in their workforce, rather than by cutting wages and conditions. This works to improve productivity and increase wages, stimulating demand. The process can also help tackle some of the problems linked to immigration and the importing of cheap labour. To achieve this, the proposals include a new Ministry of Labour responsible for promoting collective bargaining, and Sectoral Employment Commissions that would set minimum terms and conditions for each industry, through the negotiation of sector-level agreements.

The following are the key detailed proposals to be found in *A Manifesto for Labour Law*:

- A new Ministry of Labour should be established – led by a Secretary of State with a seat in the Cabinet, and mandated to represent the interests of workers in government;
- A Labour Court should be established, with specialist judges and exclusive jurisdiction to deal with all employment and labour related matters;
- A National Economic Forum should be created to encourage greater tripartite engagement in and ownership of major economic decisions and the direction of economic policy;
- The Ministry of Labour should establish Sectoral Employment Commissions with responsibilities including to promote and negotiate Sectoral Collective Agreements, set minimum terms and conditions of employment, mechanisms for the resolution of collective and individual disputes, and health and safety standards for the sector as a whole;
- Sectoral-based bargaining should be complemented by enterprise-based bargaining, applying the principle of favourability so that workers are entitled to the most favourable terms and conditions;
- Regulatory legislation should underpin collective bargaining on a range of matters such as pay, working time, including zero hours contracts,

discrimination, equality, and health and safety at work. Existing statutory standards should be universal in scope and effective in application;

- Steps should be taken to resolve more disputes without recourse to the law, under collectively agreed procedures, or summarily by labour inspectors with powers to cancel dismissal notices and order reinstatement;
- Reforms to the law on freedom of association should be made to ensure a better balance between union autonomy and union democracy, with union elections conducted in accordance with union rules and procedures;
- Recognised or representative unions should have the right to check-off facilities on request;
- More effective legislation should be introduced to stamp out blacklisting, which has a "long and pernicious pedigree in the UK". To this end, the Employment Relations Act 1999 (Blacklists) Regulations 2010 should be amended to ensure that it is always illegitimate to refuse to hire workers on grounds of past trade union activity;
- It should be made unlawful to dismiss a workplace representative except for good cause, requiring the prior approval of a senior labour inspector, whose decision should be subject to possible review;

- On the right to strike, it should be lawful for everyone to be able to take collective action with others in defence of their social and economic interests in the workplace, and for their trade unions to organise such action. The *Manifesto* calls for the repeal of the existing statutory duty to give notice of an intention to take industrial action, as well as the duty to give notice of an intention to ballot for industrial action. It proposes that a simple duty to give no less than three days strike notice would be ample;
- Unions should also be permitted to take or to call for 'secondary' or 'solidarity' industrial action in support of any other workers in dispute, including industrial action involving another employer, where the primary action is lawful. There should be a "presumption that solidarity action is lawful", because "the whole point of trade unionism is not only collective strength, but mutual support in times of trouble".
- Moreover, lawful industrial action should not be regarded as a breach of the contract of employment or service, but as a temporary suspension only. To this end, those participating in lawful collective action should have the right to be reinstated at the end of the strike, if it is their wish.

It is fairly self-evident that *A Manifesto for Labour Law* fills most, if not quite all, the gaps identified when discussing the pledges in

Labour's 2017 general election manifesto. This is fortuitous as not only does the 'wheel not need to be re-invented' but there is already some degree of sympathy for the wider set of proposals, as outlined earlier and when read in tandem with the Trade Union Freedom Bill. The task, therefore, is twofold. First, to see whether there is any need for prioritisation of particular components and, second, to work out the means by which affiliated bodies such as unions as well as Labour Party members through their Constituency Labour Parties can bring these ideas to fruition. In other words, get them adopted as Labour Party policy and use them to inform the next general election manifesto.

TRADE UNION FREEDOM BILL

John McDonnell's private members' bill, the Trade Union Freedom Bill, was twice tabled in the House of Commons in 2006 and 2008. This was after McDonnell topped the ballot for winning time within the parliamentary timetable. It arose from a centenary project looking at the 1906 Trades Disputes Act (see Ewing 2007). At its core, the Trade Union Freedom Bill comprised: (i) improved protection from dismissal and more effective remedies for workers taking part in official industrial action; (ii) simplification of the complex regulations on notices and ballots which restrict the ability of unions to organise industrial action where a clear majority of members have voted in support; and (iii) modernisation of what constitutes a trade dispute, enabling limited forms of supportive action, thereby ensuring that UK industrial action laws reflect changes in the labour market, including increased contracting out, and enabling unions to respond where employers take steps to outsource work during the course of a dispute with a view to breaking a strike.[2] Unfortunately, the first attempt to pass the Trade Union Freedom Bill was talked out by a Labour minister and former union official, Jim Fitzpatrick. On the second occasion, the Bill was put forward as an amendment to what became the Employment Act 2008 where the 'New' Labour government was assisted by Tory votes to defeat it.

CONCLUSION

Taking the 2017 general election manifesto as its starting point, a set of radical and far-reaching proposals for reforming work, employment and employment relations can be easily developed by returning to the proposals contained in the Institute of Employment Right's *A Manifesto for Labour Law* and in John Mc-Donnell's Trade Union Freedom Bill. The former is wide-ranging while the latter is particularly detailed on a narrow matter. But together they would allow for the production of version 2.0 of a Labour general election manifesto on these areas that is comprehensive and thorough in its radical ambition to transform the experience of work and employment into one that is satisfying and secure for the many and not just the few. The innovation in this approach is to combine direct state action with providing the tools to unions to allow them to do their job, at the same time as involving these unions, the representatives of 6.5 million workers, in the process of policy development.

REFERENCES

Ewing, K. (2007) (ed.) *The Right to Strike: From the Trades Disputes Act 1906 to a Trade Union Freedom Bill 2006* (Institute of Employment Rights, London).

Ewing, K., Hendy, J. and Jones, C. (2016) (eds.) *A Manifesto for Labour Law: towards a comprehensive revision of workers' rights* (Institute of Employment Rights, Liverpool).

5. SOCIAL SECURITY

Ruth Lister

MANIFESTO SUMMARY

Labour is on the side of pensioners and will guarantee the 'triple lock', increasing pensions by 2.5% a year or by the rate of increase in earnings or prices, whichever is higher. The winter fuel allowance and free bus passes will also be guaranteed as universal benefits. The pensions of citizens living overseas will be protected and the 2.5 million women who have had their pension age changed unfairly will be compensated. Labour rejects proposals to increase the pension age beyond 66 and will commission a review to look at a flexible retirement policy. It will restore confidence in the workplace pension system, specifically commissioning an immediate review of the mineworkers' pension scheme.

For those who cannot work, Labour will scrap the punitive sanctions regime, end the bedroom tax, eliminate cuts to Bereavement Support Payments and reinstate housing benefit for under 21s. Labour will reform Universal Credit, ending delays and the 'rape clause'. Labour will remove the barriers that restrict opportunities for people with disabilities, incorporating the UN Convention on the Rights of Persons with Disabilities into law. We will increase Employment and Support Allowance and Carer's Allowance, implement the Court decision on Personal Independence Payment (PIP), scrap the Work Capability and PIP assessments, end pointless reassessment for people with long term conditions and look at expanding the Access to Work programme. Labour will strengthen the 2010 Equality Act, allowing discrimination at work to be challenged. Disability hate crime and violence against women will be reported annually and national action taken to address these issues.

***

The manifesto sets the social security chapter in the context of rising poverty and (on some measures) inequality. This chapter will thus start with a brief sketch of these trends. It will then consider the functions that social security performs and the hostile climate in which it has operated in recent years. This will lead into a discussion of what is needed to achieve the very welcome commitment to "change the culture of the social security system". The chapter will set social security in the context of other policy areas it interacts with before finally commenting on specific proposals on pensions and working-age benefits. It will pay more attention to the latter because that is where the Tories have wreaked greater damage and where reform is more urgently needed.

CONTEXT AND PRINCIPLES

The Labour government's – largely unsung – success in reducing pensioner and child poverty has started to unravel after seven years of Conservative policies, although pensioner poverty remains well below its 1997-8 level. The increase in what is known as 'in-work poverty' has been particularly striking – two thirds of children in poverty now have a parent in paid work, a reminder that work is not necessarily a route out of poverty. Projections by the Institute for Fiscal Studies (IFS) and the Resolution Foundation point to a sharp increase in child and family poverty and inequality by the next decade on current policies (Hood and Waters, 2017; Corlett and Clarke, 2017).

While the relief of poverty is an important function, the manifesto reminds us that "like the NHS, our social security system is there for all of us in our time of need". It is a collective mechanism for safeguarding our economic security, particularly important at a time of widespread insecurity, thereby helping to prevent poverty, rather than just relieve it after the event. It provides shared protection against a range of risks and contingencies that we each might face during the course of our lives. It also helps to share some of the costs associated with disability, caring or raising children, thereby reducing inequality arising from differential needs. The welcome commitment to a gender audit of all policy elsewhere in the manifesto is particularly pertinent given that social security policies disproportionately affect women, but it needs to apply at the policy formulation stage and not just before implementation, as stated.

The manifesto's premise that social security is for us all is all the more important given the increased government and media vilification of 'welfare' and those reliant on it in recent years. This has fed public hostility, although this should not be overstated, and there is some evidence that it may be softening. The very use of the term social security rather than 'welfare', a break with New Labour, signals a more positive, less divisive approach. This is reflected in the chapter's emphasis on providing dignity – a central human rights principle – and its commitment to a change of culture "from one that demonises people not in work to one that is supportive and enabling". The present culture was powerfully illustrated in the film *I, Daniel Blake.* The essence of the alternative culture of citizenship needed was summed up in his final words: "I am not a shirker, a scrounger, a beggar, nor a thief...I am a man, not a dog. As such, I demand my rights. I demand you treat me with respect. I, Daniel Blake, am a citizen, nothing more and nothing less."

Daniel's call to arms points to some of the principles that should explicitly underpin a reformed social security system in order to achieve the desired change in culture. The Social Security Bill (Scotland), which begins with a set of principles, provides an example. In line with a 2012 International Labour Organisation recommendation, these principles could include "universality of protection based on social solidarity" and "respect for the rights and dignity" of recipients. Also important are: genuine economic security; a culture of prevention; a gender perspective that values contributions other than through paid work, notably care of children and older and disabled people; and engagement with those who can offer the expertise borne of the experience of living on social security.

It is important too to counteract the myth that spending on social security is 'out of control'. It is not particularly high in either a cross-national or historical context but it does have to pick up the pieces for failings in other policy areas (notably housing), covered in other chapters. Reliance on means-tested financial support for those in work could be reduced if the labour market provided more secure jobs at decent wages and if access to it were improved for marginalised groups and both individuals in couples, including through improved child care. However, because the overlap between low pay and in-work poverty is surprisingly weak, partly because wages cannot take account of family circumstances, social security, including child benefit, will always have an important role to play in preventing and reducing in-work poverty. Thus the manifesto commitment to raising the minimum wage is not of itself sufficient to tackle in-work poverty.

Social security must also be set in the context of the regressive shadow fiscal welfare state of tax reliefs and allowances. According to Andrew Harrop (2016), together they provide the same average level of support for high and low income households. This is particularly important when developing the promised new Child Poverty Strategy, given child benefit's origin in part in child tax allowances and Labour's acquiescence in the wasteful commitment of resources to raising personal tax allowances, which do little to reduce child poverty. The Tories have wrecked Labour's child poverty strategy. A renewed strategy should include:

- targets, which recognise the centrality of income;
- a cross-departmental duty on central and local government to work to achieve them;
- institutional machinery to drive and monitor the strategy.

Tax relief also needs to be part of any pensions strategy: for example, according to government figures about two-thirds of the £48 billion spent on pensions tax relief in 2014-15 benefited higher earners. A less regressive structure of reliefs could free up considerable resources, which could be used more effectively to reduce poverty and inequality.

"DIGNITY FOR PENSIONERS"

The leading commitment to pensioners is to retain the 'triple lock', which ensures that pensions rise in line with earnings, prices, or by 2.5%, whichever produces the highest increase. The triple lock, introduced by the Coalition Government, has been important in narrowing the wide gap that had opened up between pensions and wages following the Tories' abolition of the link with earnings in 1980. Although the 'triple' element is unlikely to make much difference in the near future with the rise in inflation, it is an expensive longer term commitment.

Growing calls for its abandonment, as typical pensioner household incomes now outstrip non-pensioners', highlight the need
to debate its future. The 2.5% was an arbitrary figure whereas
there is a logic to some form of a double earnings/prices lock
(as operated for a period previously). One option, supported by
the Commons Work and Pensions Committee, is a 'smoothed
earnings link', which maintains pensions at an agreed percentage
of average earnings, while ensuring that they do not lose value
at times when inflation outstrips earnings. If the triple lock were
to be abandoned for some form of double lock, consideration
would be needed as to how to protect older pensioners, mainly
women, still reliant on the old basic state pension. They are still
at a high risk of poverty despite the overall risk among pensioners having fallen below that of people below pension age. At the
very least, more could be done to raise take-up of pension credit
from its present level of 62%.

At the other end of the pensioner age scale, the manifesto
promises some form of transitional protection for the 'Waspi'
women (Women Against State Pension Inequality) whose campaign has highlighted their shock at the inadequate notification
of the rise in their state pension age. Although it is generally
accepted that equalisation of the pension age is fair, how it was
done has caused considerable heartache. As the pension age is
due to rise still further for both women and men, the manifesto
promises a review to consider a flexible retirement policy, which
would take account of variations in life expectancy – hopefully, with some emphasis on *healthy* life expectancy – and "the

arduous conditions of some work". In promising to "restore confidence in the workplace pension system," there seems to be an acceptance that pensioners will be left to the mercies of the private sector for any provision above the new flat rate single tier state pension. Any review of pensions might want to reconsider this because, as Fran Bennett among others has argued, "we thus lose the ability to proactively shape earnings-related provision to reflect social priorities such as redistributing towards the lower paid and those taking time out for caring" (Letter to *Financial Times*, 1st June 2017).

The endorsement of universal winter fuel allowances and free bus passes is welcome. Universality ensures those eligible will receive them without off-putting and divisive means-testing. While these benefits are not core social security provisions, they encourage pensioners not to skimp on heating and to maintain mobility and social contacts respectively, both important on health grounds. However, there is a case for targeting the fuel allowance more precisely by age so that it would be payable only from, say, age 75, with the exception of those receiving disability benefits. This might reduce the perennial grumbling about it being paid to those 'do not need it'.

"DIGNITY FOR THOSE WHO CANNOT WORK"

Welcome as the commitment to the dignity of those who cannot work is, the title of this section is misleading because it plays into the belief that social security is not important for people in work as well. Yet low income working families have been among the main victims of Tory social security cuts – projected to rise to over £14 billion a year by 2021 – and simply raising the minimum wage will not compensate them. Despite the positive tone, this is a disappointing section. The manifesto's accompanying funding document commits only an additional £4 billion a year to working-age social security – a fraction of the cuts it has suffered. Women, children and some minority ethnic groups will be disproportionately affected.

More positively, the manifesto does promise to reverse most, though not all, of the damage done to disability benefits in terms of both rates and eligibility rules and to overhaul the much-criticised assessments governing entitlement to employment and support allowance (ESA) and personal independence payments. The commitment to incorporate into law the UN Convention on the Rights of Persons with Disabilities is very welcome, especially given the damning verdict of a 2016 UN Inquiry that the cuts amounted to a systematic violation of disabled people's rights. As well as reversing cuts, the manifesto promises a long overdue increase in carer's allowance to align it with jobseeker's allowance. A commissioned report into expanding the Access to Work programme is also planned. This needs to be part of a wider review, in consultation with disabled people and their organisations, aimed at providing high-quality, impairment-specific employment services.

The other clear, funded, commitments are to:

- scrap the highly unpopular bedroom tax, which has caused considerable hardship while doing little to release under-occupied housing;
- reinstate housing benefit for under-21s. Its removal in April 2017 has been associated with widespread fears that it will further increase homelessness; and
- reverse £100 million worth of cuts to bereavement support, which have significantly reduced its duration at the expense of bereaved partners with young children.

In addition, the chapter pledges to "scrap the punitive sanctions regime". This should both help to achieve the promised culture change and reduce destitution and reliance on food banks, which numerous studies have linked to sanctions. The sanctions rate has now fallen again in the face of the outcry against widespread indiscriminate penalties, for which there is limited evidence of effectiveness. Nevertheless, sanctions can still be applied for up to three years with inadequate protection through hardship payments, which have been made more restrictive and recoverable. The extension of conditionality to more groups, in particular lone parents with young children, and under universal credit to partners with children, has widened the sanctions net. The next, unprecedented, step is its application to people in work receiving universal credit (UC) who are deemed to have insufficient

earnings. It is not clear whether Labour would scrap this potentially highly damaging new rule, currently being piloted.

This is one of a number of question marks hanging over a
promise to "reform and redesign" UC. According to the Resolution Foundation, the £2 billion earmarked in the funding document for a review of how best to reverse cuts in UC would cover
only about two-fifths of them (Finch, 2017). There is a clear commitment to end the 'rape clause', which presumably means the
unfair rule limiting UC and tax credit payments to two children
in a family, from which it provides exemption. As the manifesto
points out, this – and also the big cuts to UC work allowances,
which set the maximum earnings allowed before benefit starts
to be withdrawn – will increase child poverty. However, even
though the manifesto dubs the work allowance cuts "an attack
on low income families", there is no clear commitment to reverse
them. Nor is there acknowledgement of widespread calls for a
second earner work allowance, which would encourage second
earners, mainly women still, into paid work and thereby help reduce in-work child poverty. A promise to repeal cuts in the UC
limited capability for work element needs to be part of a wider
scrutiny of the adequacy of UC support for disabled people.

The other clear UC commitment is to end the current six-
week wait – often longer in practice – for the first payment. As
UC is rolled out more widely, evidence is growing of debt, arrears
and the general hardship this causes. This needs to be addressed
not only by abolishing the seven-day waiting period before eligibility starts but also by reviewing the ideologically motivated

switch from fortnightly to monthly payments and assessment. The Women's Budget Group and others have warned that this will have a disproportionate impact on mothers struggling with everyday budgeting. There are also concerns that women, in particular those subject to domestic violence, could be adversely affected by the payment of UC into a single bank account. Although no mention is made of this, it should be included in the promised review of UC, which needs to be wide-ranging.

The two most glaring omissions in the manifesto's commitments to reverse cuts are the benefit cap and freeze in working age benefit levels. Debbie Abrahams, Shadow Work and Pensions Secretary, has subsequently (on *The Andrew Marr Show*, 25th June 2017) indicated a willingness to look at how to fund abolition of the cap. This is welcome news because previously there had been a refusal to oppose the principle of the cap and argue that benefit entitlement should not be reduced below the level Parliament has deemed is necessary to meet basic needs. The Government's attempt to justify the breach of this principle on grounds of fairness between those in and out of work was undermined by its refusal to include in-work benefits in the equation. The numbers affected by the cap at any one time, although relatively low, have increased more than threefold to 68,000 since the level was arbitrarily lowered in November 2016,with a larger proportion (approximately half) now losing more than £50 a week. In the judgment on a recent successful appeal to the High Court against the cap's imposition on lone parents with children aged under two (which the government plans to challenge), the

judge concluded "real misery is being caused to no good purpose". Should it be deemed impossible to abolish the cap immediately, acceptance of the High Court decision, the restoration
of the cap's original level and the exclusion from it of children's
benefits also paid in work would at least mitigate significantly its
damaging impact on child poverty.

The complete failure even to mention the freeze of most
working-age and children's benefits is extraordinary. The four-
year freeze, coming on top of below-inflation increases under the
Coalition, has been identified as one of the main drivers of the
anticipated increase in child poverty and inequality mentioned
above, affecting those on low incomes in and out of work. Already, the real increases in child benefit under Labour have been
undone: it is set to lose 23% of its value this decade. Jobseeker's allowance is projected to be reduced to its lowest value since
1991-92 (Whittaker, 2017). The cumulative impact of the freeze
cannot be ignored if we are serious about tackling child poverty
and inequality. Even former Secretary of State Iain Duncan Smith
has acknowledged that this needs reviewing in the light of higher
than anticipated inflation. Yet Labour had no coherent response
when interrogated on it during the election campaign.

A LONGER-TERM STRATEGY

It is understandable that the manifesto focused on reversing cuts
and this will clearly be the immediate priority for an incoming

government. But there also needs to be some indication of a longer-term vision. The growing residualisation of social security, as successive governments have increased reliance on means-testing, means that increasingly it is not seen as 'there for all of us'. We need a more fundamental review of social security and its functions with the aim of providing genuine economic security for all, with minimal reliance on divisive and inefficient means-testing. A first step could be to abolish the time limit on contributory ESA for the work-related activity group, introduced by the Tories, and restore contributory support for unemployed people to twelve months. In the longer term the two main options to consider are: a revitalised, more inclusive contributory social insurance scheme or a universal basic income, with a third option, a participation income as a variant (see Lister, 2016; Harrop 2016).

CONCLUSION

The manifesto has rightly been praised for offering a radical, hopeful vision of a more equal, fairer society, which offers security and dignity to all. Yet, despite its welcome positive tone, the chapter on one of the key building blocks of such a vision is depressingly inadequate to the task. Indeed, by ignoring one of the most damaging of the Tories' social security cuts, it is effectively acquiescing in a further increase in child poverty and inequality. The next manifesto must include a coherent short- and longer-term strategy for tackling and preventing poverty and inequality, in which social security reform plays a central role.

The author wishes to thank Fran Bennett, Geoff Fimister, Patricia Hollis, Jonquil Lowe, Debbie Price and Maeve Sherlock for their helpful input.

REFERENCES

Corlett, Adam, Clarke, Stephen, *Living Standards* (Resolution Foundation, London: 2017).

Corlett, Adam, Clarke, Stephen and Tomlinson, Dan, *The Living Standards Audit* (Resolution Foundation, London: 2017).

Finch, David, *Still just about managing?* (Resolution Foundation, London: 2017).

Harrop, Andrew, *For Us All*, (Fabian Society, London: 2016).

Hood, Andrew and Waters, Tom, *Living Standards, Poverty and Inequality in the UK: 2016-17 to 2021-22* (IFS, London: 2017).

Lister, Ruth 'Putting the security back into social security' in Lisa Nandy, Caroline Lucas and Chris Bowers (eds) *The Alternative* (Biteback, London: 2016).

Whittacker, Matt, *Ending Austerity?* (Resolution Foundation, London: 2017).

6. SECURE HOMES FOR ALL[1]

Stuart Hodkinson

MANIFESTO SUMMARY

Britain has a housing crisis – of supply and affordability. Labour will invest to build over a million new homes, with 100,000 affordable council or housing association homes in the next Parliament, overseen by a new Department for Housing. We will overhaul housing delivery and give councils new powers to build, prioritising brownfield sites, but also beginning a new generation of New Towns. Labour will also insulate more homes, consult on new rules on minimum space standards, ensure that local plans address the need for older people's housing and keep the Land Registry in public hands.

Labour will build thousands more low-cost homes for first time buyers and guarantee Help to Buy funding until 2027. It will give leaseholders security from rip-off ground rents and end the routine use of leaseholds in new developments. For private renters, there will be controls of rent rises and more secure tenancies, with three year tenancies becoming the norm. Letting agency fees will be banned and tenants given new consumer rights, with new minimum standards on housing fitness. Housing benefit will be restored for 18 to 21 year olds.

Labour will remove restrictions on councils building homes and start a major council house building programme. The Bedroom Tax will be scrapped and the right to buy policy suspended to protect affordable homes. To tackle homelessness, Labour will set out a new national plan to end rough sleeping and safeguard homeless hostels and other supported housing.

***

Labour's manifesto was unlike any other for decades, especially in the radical spirit of its slogan "Secure homes for all". Nevertheless, it bore the hallmarks of an ideologically-divided Parliamentary Party, with socialist rhetoric masking a failure to take on the neoliberal model of speculative housebuilding and wealth extraction from property ownership. The timidity of Labour's approach to the housing crisis was exposed a month after the 2017 General Election by the appalling Grenfell Tower fire disaster in London, in which at least 80 people died from the deadly consequence of privatisation, deregulation, and austerity. With the neoliberal consensus on housing clearly fractured by Grenfell, the next Labour manifesto must embrace a more transformational agenda to achieve safe and secure homes for all.

THE CRISIS OF HOUSING INSECURITY

The 2017 General Election was contested against the background of an acute and worsening crisis of housing insecurity after seven years of cruel Conservative austerity policies that have hit the poorest households and communities hardest. Despite historically low mortgage interest rates, access to home ownership is increasingly blocked off across England by the lowest peacetime building output for over 90 years and house prices outstripping average incomes. If this continues, by 2020, the projected average house price of £270,000 will leave typical first time buyers needing to earn £64,000 a year and have a deposit of £46,000 (Shelter, 2016). Priced out of home ownership, and unable to access social housing after decades of privatisation, today's Generation Rent (Walker, 2012) is fuelling the remarkable resurgence of the private rental sector which has more than doubled in the past two decades and on present trends will soon house one in every four households (Knight Frank, 2017).

With demand overtaking supply, average private rents have risen to 35% of household income, compared to 18% for average mortgage costs, and almost one in seven private renters spends over half their income on rent (LGA, 2017). Increasingly, tenants are in serious arrears, and a record number of official evictions are taking place, up by a third between 2010 and 2016 to over 40,000 a year. Private landlords are exploiting the-called "no fault" repossession route under section 21 of the Housing Act 1988 to eject tenants once their six months are up and re-let at higher rents (Clarke et al, 2017). No wonder homelessness has risen by nearly 60% since 2009 (Shelter, 2017), pushing over 120,000 children into temporary accommodation (LGA, 2017).

Driving this trend is the Conservatives' welfare reform programme. A benefit cap has hit all out of work households and couples working up to 23 hours a week, with housing benefit the first payment to be cut once the cap is breached. Social tenants deemed to be under-occupying their homes – even though most have no choice – have been hit by the Bedroom Tax, reducing their housing benefit on average by more than £15 a week nationally and £21 a week in London (DWP, 2017). Nearly 90% of council tenants on the Universal Credit system are in rent arrears (National Federation of ALMOs, 2017). Cuts to housing benefit for private renters have drastically shrunk the choice of accommodation available to low-income households and created a growing affordability gap between benefit payments and rents. Shelter (2017) predicts that by 2020 over a million households in Britain could be put at risk of homelessness unless the freeze on housing benefit levels is lifted.

This housing insecurity crisis is most acute in London where average house prices and rents are more than double the rest of England and almost 40% of all evictions take place. With slashed council budgets meeting high real estate values, many London urban authorities, mostly Labour-run, are being pressured some only too willingly – to cash in by offering public land for private development. Under the bogus guise of 'regeneration', increasing numbers of council estates are being earmarked for demolition and sale to large real estate investors who build almost exclusively private housing for sale or rent, accelerating the gentrification of inner London. When combined with welfare cuts and the growing shortage of social housing, an unprecedented social cleansing is in motion that saw just under 20,000 London households in temporary accommodation moved to another local authority area in 2016, most to the South East and East of England, but some as far away as Birmingham (*Guardian*, 2017; Hardy and Gillespie, 2016; Watt, 2017).

This 'social cleansing' is driven by the Conservative government's determination to create an urban order in which one's postcode is dictated only by one's wealth. But it is also the long-term consequence of neoliberal policies that have rendered increasing numbers of people structurally invested in the reproduction of unaffordable housing so that personal asset wealth can replace the retreating welfare state as a source of future and current consumption.

LABOUR'S RADICAL AMBITION: SECURE HOMES FOR ALL

Against this crisis, Labour's slogan of "Secure homes for all" was a magnificent marker of radical intent to make housing a universal right, not a class privilege. New Labour would only commit to ensuring housing security for owner-occupiers (The Labour Party, 1997), and its promises to tackle housing problems always came with a commitment to be tough on welfare claimants or embracing privatisation. This manifesto offered change unconditionally, viewing home as "the heart of all of our lives... the foundation on which we raise our families, the bedrock for our dreams and aspirations" (The Labour Party, 2017). Such foundations imply legally protected, geographically stable, and physically safe housing for everyone, and the manifesto – and its accompanying New Deal on Housing policy document – contained important policies to this end.

Homeowners were offered a new "Homeowner Guarantee" that unemployment or reduced hours would not lead to repossession, by speeding up access to mortgage interest loan support and improving support for low-paid homeowners. In common with other parties, Labour would also legislate to protect leaseholders from unfair 'ground rent' increases buried in leases of many new developments, rendering the property increasingly unaffordable and unsellable.[2] For renters, statutory secure council tenancies, abolished by the Tories, would be restored, and the manifesto kept Labour's 2015 promise of re-regulating private landlords. Three year secure private tenancies would be the new legal norm (not six months as at present), with tenants able to give two months' notice. Rent rises would be capped by inflation, all landlords would be licensed and councils would have new powers to name, shame and levy fines of £100,000 on those failing to meet new legal minimum fitness standards in a sector where over 400,000 families with children live in homes that fail basic standards (Shelter, 2014). Private tenants would also be given new consumer rights to challenge bad landlords letting out dangerous or substandard homes without fear of retaliatory eviction.

Taken together, these reforms would reduce housing insecurity and the power of monopoly landlordism, but they need to be more ambitious if they are to achieve their goals. The next manifesto should introduce the longstanding idea of a 'right to sell' in which home owners who can no longer cope could sell their home to the council and take up a secure council tenancy (Labour Housing Group, 1984). Private tenants should receive a statutory five year tenancy with an automatic right of renewal linked to satisfactory fitness and safety inspections and section 21 of the 1988 Housing Act should be reformed to end no-fault evictions.

Far less promoted but of equal significance was Labour's commitment to redefine affordable housing as a function of income, not market price. So instead of taxpayers subsidising a 20% discount on so-called Starter Homes for first-time buyers, worth £450,000 in London and £250,000 elsewhere, Labour would invest in 100,000 FirstBuy Homes where mortgage costs would never exceed a third of average local incomes in perpetuity for future buyers. Similarly, the Orwellian-branded 'Affordable Rent' programme of up to 80% market rents would be replaced by Living Rent homes let at a third of local incomes to help private renters save for a deposit on a first home. And, in a gesture against international investor speculation, Labour would introduce a 'first dibs' rule on new housing in which developers would be forced to market new homes to local first-time buyers first, not to overseas buyers or those with no connection to the area.

Yet on what Corbyn himself argued was the key driver of housing insecurity for all tenures – austerity cuts to the benefits system – Labour was seriously timid, promising only to "end the worst excesses of the Conservative government's changes" such as scrapping the punitive sanctions regime and Bedroom Tax, and reinstating Housing Benefit for under-21s. There was no mention of reversing cuts to Local Housing Allowance for private renters or of unfreezing benefit levels to plug the growing affordability gap between falling benefits in real terms and rising rents. Whereas the Lib Dems proposed to match housing benefit to average local rents so that a family could afford "to pay their housing costs no matter where they live" (Liberal Democrats, 2017), Labour would only offer a review of social security support for housing costs.

The next manifesto must restore the link between income and housing costs within a wider rent restructuring strategy for both social and private rental sectors in which rents are gradually recalibrated to an affordable local income level set by the Low Pay Commission, which currently sets the national minimum wage. It must also reverse the anti-homeless legislation of the Coalition's 2011 Localism Act, reinstate the right of the statutory homeless in England to a secure social housing tenancy, and make all out-of-borough placements illegal, not just those where the local authority fails to properly search for local temporary accommodation. This would be a major barrier to displacement in and out of London, with councils currently free to determine which homeless households are prioritised for social housing and which will be pushed into poor quality private housing on short term tenancies miles away.

NEW DEAL OR SAME DEAL? A MISSED OPPORTUNITY FOR REAL CHANGE

One of the key tests for the manifesto was how it would tackle the structural dysfunctionality of the supply-side. Recent research shows that because of the current low building rate, England must double the annual supply of new homes, and quadruple this rate in London, just to catch up with new household formation (McDonald and Whitehead, 2015). Corbyn himself has blamed the supply side crisis on previous governments for allowing for-profit landowners and developers to gain control of housebuilding and land supply, and removing not-for-profit actors from that role.

At first glance, therefore, Labour's renewed commitment to council housing augured well. Labour vowed to suspend the right to buy (RTB) in England (it is already suspended in Wales and abolished in Scotland under devolution) until a council could legitimately replace every home sold like-for-like. This was long overdue: the RTB with its generous taxpayer discounts to help tenants buy their council home has caused the loss of 1.82 million council homes in England alone since 1979, of which a staggering 40% are now in the private rented sector (House of

Commons, 2016). Labour would also lift current borrowing caps on councils' housing revenue accounts to help "begin the biggest council building programme for at least 30 years". The political significance of this shift should not be underestimated: such was the Blairite hostility to council housing, New Labour built fewer council homes over its 13 years in power than Thatcher built in her final year in office.

Nevertheless, the manifesto's commitments on council housing were a pale imitation of Corbyn's 2016 leadership pitch to build half a million council homes and end RTB. Instead, Labour promised a more ambiguous 100,000 council and housing association homes a year, for both rent and sale. Nor was there a direct commitment to restore government subsidy without which councils' renewed powers to borrow would be unlikely to generate more than 40,000 council homes a year and only then if they diverted investment away from existing homes (NFH, 2012). The RTB itself would not be reformed, meaning no rolling-back of the Tories' disastrous increases to discounts from £38,000 under Labour to £104,900 in London and £78,600 elsewhere, currently generating the loss of around 12,000 council homes a year. Nor was any promise made to scrap councils' future obligation to sell off their most valuable council houses on the open market when vacant.

Overall, the manifesto's proposals posed a real risk that any net additional supply of new council homes would be largely eroded by like-for-like replacements for existing units sold. This would offer Labour councils little alternative than to carry on setting up Local Housing Companies outside of the housing revenue account, to demolish existing council housing and become speculative developers of private housing for sale and rent. The next manifesto must restore government subsidy to support the construction of 100,000 net additional council homes a year, scrap all current estate regeneration schemes in favour of refurbishment and ballots for residents on development plans, and abolish the RTB and high-value council house sales. It should also reverse all deregulatory measures in the Housing and Planning Act 2016, especially restoring the requirement for housing associations to gain regulatory consent when using their housing stock as collateral to help prevent risky borrowing that is driving some social landlords into bankruptcy, threatening the stock of social housing. Instead, Labour should create a new Right to Own based on Nevitt's (1971) "communal tenant ownership" vision in which all social tenants are made joint-legal owners of social housing. This would give them rights to security of tenure, to improve their homes, to be represented on local housing management committees, and to enjoy the lowest possible rents based on collective sharing of costs and risks via the state and foregoing the financial stake in the capital value of their homes.

The failure to be much bolder on the RTB and financing new council housing underscored the manifesto's failure to take on the neoliberal model of speculative housebuilding and wealth extraction from property and land ownership. Labour continued the dangerous fetishism of 'aspirational home ownership', proclaiming home ownership as "special" and key to closing the "gulf in wealth and opportunity within and between generations". The commitment to maintain the Help to Buy programme until at least 2027 reconfirms the disastrous long-term cross-party consensus on subsidising home ownership in ways that boost demand without increasing supply, and artificially inflate house prices while doing little to increase affordability. The target of a million new homes by 2022 would also be largely aimed at building homes to buy and would rely on the very same top ten private builders that currently control around half of all housing production (compared to just 9% in 1960) and have used their producer power and land banks to deliberately restrict the flow and increase the price of new housing so as to make huge profits since 2010 (Archer and Cole, 2016).

The manifesto offered nothing concrete to tackle house price inflation and the dominance of these rentier capitalists, just frustratingly vague promises to negotiate better deals and give local authorities 'use it or lose it' powers where development is being held up "without good cause". Instead, just as under the Conservatives, these very same commercial developers would be given access to discounted public land.

A future Labour government should prioritise public land for council housing, make clear that house price inflation should no longer be a government policy aim and adopt the New Economics Foundation's recommendations for deflating the UK housing market, including abolishing Help to Buy and all demand subsidies (for example, Mortgage Interest Relief) for home ownership, re-regulating mortgage lending to phase out risky and destabilising loans, and raising capital gains taxes on the excess profits of developers and strategic land promoters (Fraser, 2017) to fund its council house building programme (NEF, 2015). In addition, Labour should set up a Land Commission charged with restructuring the dysfunctional land market, setting up a Land Value Tax to capture unearned income from speculation and incentivise productive investment, and compulsorily purchasing new land for housing development at a fair price that does not reward unearned income.

This refusal to subvert private property was reflected in Labour's conservative stance on tackling the scandal of empty and under-occupied homes in the owner-occupied sector. There are currently around 600,000 empty homes in England, of which 246,540 dwellings are classed as second homes and a further 200,000 as long-term vacant (over six months). The manifesto promised councils stronger powers to take over and rent out empty homes, and charge a 300% empty homes premium on properties empty for more than a year, compared to the current rate of 150% after two years. But in many parts of southern England, property values are increasing at a faster rate than the extra tax they would incur, and councils appear unwilling to use their existing tax premium powers with fewer than one in three of the 200,000 homes eligible subject to the 150% council tax in 2016 (see DCLG Local Authority Council Tax base England, 2016).

A future Labour government should make its empty homes premium compulsory with a ratchet mechanism, so that the council tax doubles every six months a home is left empty, and include second homes or holiday homes in this. It should also commit to the decriminalisation of squatting brought in under the Coalition, which has put homeless people in jail while the real criminals who leave homes empty are rewarded with capital gains. Finally, Labour must grasp the nettle of the country's real under-occupation problem in the homeowner sector where 52% of homes have spare bedrooms and recent research found that two-thirds of over-55s with at least two spare bedrooms would prefer to move to a smaller property, freeing 2.6 million family homes and 7.7 million un-used bedrooms (Legal and General, 2015). If Labour combines a council building programme to create the right mix of homes, and the tax and welfare system to incentivise these homeowners to downsize to them, the housing crisis could be solved within a decade.

AFTER GRENFELL: SAFE AND SECURE HOMES FOR ALL!

Labour's commitment to secure homes for all marks a major breakthrough in moving the Party towards a position that has long been a standard bearer for the left – the universal right to housing. But for all its radical rhetoric, the manifesto was a missed opportunity to change the narrative of the problem and thus create oxygen for more radical ideas around which social movements can mobilise. In truth, the headline-grabbing promises on new council housing and regulating private landlords sugar-coated a largely traditional Labour housing programme that would leave the speculators in charge.

Since the election, however, housing has moved centre-stage with the events of 14 June 2017, when Grenfell Tower, a high-rise council block of flats in the country's richest borough, Kensington and Chelsea, caught fire after a fridge exploded. Within minutes, the fire had spread rapidly through the newly-fitted cladding to the entire 24 floors, eventually killing a suspected 100 people and leaving surviving households homeless. Within hours, it emerged that its residents had warned of shoddy and unsafe work over many years, and predicted that only a devastating fire would make the Conservative-run local authority and its arms-length housing management company listen. Over the next days, other tower blocks' cladding across the country was deemed unsafe, austerity was being blamed for cost-cutting exercises to Grenfell that saw the original cladding replaced with a flammable product, and questions were focusing on how such unsafe design and works could have passed building control inspections.

In truth, the Grenfell disaster grew out of decades of industry deregulation and cuts to local authorities' building control departments under both the Conservatives and New Labour. Consequently, work done by almost exclusively private contractors and their long, badly monitored sub-contracting chains is rarely properly checked. Fire safety has been overlooked in housing law for decades. The Housing Act 2004 effectively abolished the legal minimum fitness standard for rental housing and by making local authorities solely responsible for inspection and enforcement in relation to relevant fire hazards, it reduced tenants' already limited rights to enforce safety, and made council tenants such as those living in Grenfell virtually powerless, as local housing authorities are unable to enforce against themselves (Huckle, 2017).

Post-Grenfell, better quality housing is no longer about insulation or regulating private landlords, as the Labour manifesto intended. Instead, we need to overhaul all building and fire safety regulations, regulate the construction industry and ensure that standards are enforced for all existing and new homes of all tenures. This means ending the disastrous regime of self-regulation and investing in a National Housing Fitness and Safety Inspectorate, independent of all social and private landlords, construction companies and industry bodies, with legal powers to inspect and enforce regulations. Tenants and purchasers of homes should have direct access to this Inspectorate to raise concerns about the safety and fitness of their homes and the Inspectorate should investigate independently of the landlord or developer, and enforce repair work without the occupier having to go to court. The costs of the Inspectorate could be met by fines levied against the landlord or developer and if they wanted to contest this, they would have to take the Inspectorate, not the occupier, to court. Funding should be available to ensure that residents can set up their own tenants' and residents' associations independent of local authorities or private landlords.

The Grenfell Tower disaster has dramatically shifted the political terrain of housing to the left and Labour must now seize the initiative and set out a radical programme for ensuring that all homes are both secure and safe to live in and that residents' voices are democratically enshrined in housing governance.

REFERENCES

Archer, T and Cole, I, *Profits before Volume? Major housebuilders and the crisis of housing supply*, (Sheffield Hallam University: 2016) https://www4.shu.ac.uk/research/cresr/sites/shu.ac.uk/files/profits-before-volume-housebuilders-crisis-housing-supply.pdf

Clarke, A et al, *Poverty, evictions and forced moves* (Joseph Rowntree Foundation, York: 2017). http://www.cchpr.landecon.cam.ac.uk/Projects/Start-Year/2016/Poverty-evictions-and-forced-moves/OutputTemplate/DownloadTemplate

DCLG, *Local Authority Council Tax base England 2016* (DCLG: 2016), https://www.gov.uk/government/statistics/council-taxbase-2016-in-england

DCLG, *English Household Survey 2016* (DCLG: 2017) https://www.gov.uk/government/statistics/english-housing-survey-2015-to-2016-headline-report

DWP, *Housing Benefit Caseload Data, May 2017* (DWP, Stat-Xplore, 2017), https://www.gov.uk/government/uploads/

system/uploads/attachment_data/file/499812/housing-benefit-caseload-data-to-May-2017.xls

Empty Homes Agency, Empty Homes in England (2016) http://www.emptyhomes.com/assets/empty-homes-in-england-final-september-2016.pdf

Fraser, I, The modern-day barons: inside the murky underbelly of land promotion (*The Telegraph*, 5 August 2017), http://www.telegraph.co.uk/business/2017/08/05/modern-day-barons-inside-murky-underbelly-land-promotion/

Hardy, K, and Gillespie, T, Homelessness, health and housing: participatory action research in East London, (Feminist Review Trust, University of Leeds: 2016).

House of Commons Select Committee Comunities and Local Government, Housing associations and the Right to Buy, (Housing of Commons, 2016) https://publications.parliament.uk/pa/cm201516/cmselect/cmcomloc/370/37002.htm

Huckle, T, Grenfell Tower – a different perspective (New Law Journal, Vol. 167: 7753: 2017) www.newlawjournal.co.uk/content/grenfell-tower-different-perspective

Knight Frank, Multihousing 2017: PRS Research, (2017) https://kfcontent.blob.core.windows.net/research/707/documents/en/the-uk-tenant-survey-2017-4743.pdf

Labour Housing Group, *Right to a Home* (Spokesman, London: 1984).

Labour Party, The, *Labour's New Deal on Housing* (The Labour Party, London: 2017).

Labour Party, The, *New Labour because Britain Deserves Better* (The Labour Party, London: 1997).

Legal and General (2015), Last Time Buyers https://www.legalandgeneralgroup.com/assets/portal/files/pdf_175.pdf

Liberal Democrats, The, *Change Britain's Future Liberal Democrat Manifesto* (2017), https://www.libdems.org.uk/manifesto

Local Government Association, *Housing Our Homeless Households* (LGA, London: 2017) https://www.local.gov.uk/sites/default/files/documents/5.12%20HOUSING%20AND%20HOMELESSNESS_v08_4.pdf

LGA, Rental logjam as one in seven private renters spend half their income on rent: LGA analysis

https://www.local.gov.uk/about/news/rental-logjam-one-seven-private-renters-spend-half-their-income-rent-lga-analysis

McDonald, N and Whitehead, C, New estimates of housing requirements in England, 2012 to 2037 (*Town & Country Planning Tomorrow Series* Paper 17: 2015) https://www.tcpa.org.uk/Handlers/Download.ashx?IDMF=7e5d434f-6d73-46e5-adee-11b02606933e

Ministry of Justice, Mortgage and landlord possession statistical tables: January to March 2017, https://www.gov.uk/

government/statistics/mortgage-and-landlord-possession-
statistics-january-to-march-2017

National Federation of ALMOs (NFA), Pause for thought,
Measuring the impact of Welfare Reform on tenants and
landlords – 2017 Survey results, (2017) http://www.almos.
org.uk/include/getDoc.php?did=7944&fid=9326

New Economics Foundation (NEF), Written evidence to the
Inquiry into the Economics of the UK Housing Market
(NEF, London: 2015) http://b.3cdn.net/nefoundation/
b6fba96872fa15e8c1_pym6bp6x6.pdf

Nevitt, D A, *Fair deal for householders* (Fabian Society, London:
1971).

NFA, Let's get building The case for local authority investment in
rented homes to help drive economic growth, 2012, http://
www.almos.org.uk/document?id=5300

Shelter, 'First time buyers will need £64,000 salary to afford an
average home by 2020', (Shelter, London: 2016), https://
england.shelter.org.uk/media/press_releases/articles/
first_time_buyers_will_need_64,000_salary_to_afford_an_
average_home_by_2020,_warns_shelter

Shelter, Shut Out: Households at put at risk of homelessness
by the housing benefit freeze (Shelter, London: 2017),
https://england.shelter.org.uk/__data/assets/pdf_
file/0005/1391675/LHA_analysis_note_FINAL.pdf

Turner, A, UK's homeless families forced to wave goodbye to their support network (*The Guardian*: 2017) https://www.theguardian.com/society/2017/apr/05/homeless-families-housed-out-of-area-growing-problem

Walker, T, No place like home: the generation who can't afford to buy, (*The Independent*: 2012).

http://www.independent.co.uk/property/house-and-home/no-place-like-home-the-generation-who-cant-afford-to-buy-1921781.html

Watt, P, Gendering the right to housing in the city: Homeless female lone parents in post-Olympics austerity East London (*Cities*, 2017).

7. HEALTHCARE FOR ALL

Allyson Pollock

MANIFESTO SUMMARY

Labour will invest in the NHS to ensure patients get world-class quality care, guaranteeing the standards to which patients are legally entitled under the NHS constitution. We will work towards a new model of community care, increasing funding to GP services, halting pharmacy cuts and reviewing provision. We will tackle the problem of rationing of services, ensuring all NHS patients get fast access to the most effective new treatments, based on value-for-money agreements with pharmaceutical companies. We will ensure that everyone with a long-term condition will have the right to a specialised care plan and guarantee high-quality, personalised care for people approaching the end of their life. Labour will ensure that NHS England completes the trial programme to provide PrEP as quickly as possible, and fully roll out the treatment to high-risk groups to help reduce HIV infection. Labour will fund free parking in NHS England by increasing the tax on private insurance premiums.

We will take action to reduce infant deaths and ensure all families who lose a baby receive appropriate bereavement support. We will aim to make our children the healthiest in the world, breaking the scandalous link between child ill-health and poverty. We will introduce a new Index of Child Health to measure progress and report annually against the key indicators. A new £250 million Children's Health Fund will support this alongside increased numbers of school nurses and health visitors. Within 100 days, we will publish a new childhood obesity strategy, with proposals on advertising and food labelling. Labour will implement the Soft Drinks Industry Levy, commonly known as the 'sugar tax', a strategy for the children of alcoholics and a Tobacco Control Plan, focusing on issues of mental health and young smokers.

Labour will address historic public health injustices, with a public enquiry into contaminated blood. We will also hold a public inquiry into medicines, including Valproate, medical devices and medical products licensing and regulation. We remain committed to improve sexual health services, especially HIV.

As part of a long-term workforce plan, Labour will scrap the NHS pay cap and put pay back into the hands of the independent pay review body. We will re-introduce funding for health-related degrees and invest in the career-long training of doctors. We will immediately guarantee the rights of EU health and care staff, support NHS staff who speak up in support of patient standards and make it an aggravated criminal offence to attack NHS staff.

Labour will put £30 billion extra funding into the NHS over the next Parliament through increasing income tax for the top 5% and tax on private medical insurance and we will free up resources by halving the fees paid to management consultants. We will boost capital funding and introduce a new Office for Budget Responsibility for Health to oversee spending. We will halt the Sustainability and Transformation Plans that close services and involve local people in redrawing plans based on patient need, supported by a new quality regulator. Labour will repeal the Health and Social Care Act, reverse privatisation and give the Secretary of State overall NHS responsibility, with a new legal duty to ensure excess private profits are not made.

We will build a National Care Service for England, in partnership with the NHS, increasing social care budgets by a further £8 billion over five years, allowing implementation of the principles of the Ethical Care Charter. Labour will also increase the Carer's Allowance for unpaid full-time carers to align it with the Jobseeker's Allowance. This service will require an additional £3 billion of public funds a year, enough to place a maximum limit on lifetime personal contributions to care costs, raise the asset threshold below which people are entitled to state support and provide free end-of-life care.

Labour will ring-fence mental health budgets and stop the scandal of children being treated on adult mental health wards or people being sent away from their support networks. Labour will increase mental health resources for young people, with counselling in all secondary schools. We will ask the National Institute for Health and Care Excellence to look at widening the range of therapies on offer.

***

The 2017 Labour manifesto for health, like the road to hell, is paved with good intentions. Its pledges include improving children's and mental health services, more funding for NHS and social care, tackling obesity and other public health prevention initiatives. However, unlike the Beveridge report of 1942, which considered the social determinants of health in the round, with its plan to slay the five giants of want, disease, ignorance, idleness and squalor, this manifesto for health has no public health framework. It is puzzling to see the issues of tackling unhealthy foods, obesity, physical activity, smoking and alcohol tucked under public health and the NHS, when what is required is an appreciation of the wider health political economy and the roles of industry and poverty. Redistributive policies are absent as are legislative actions, apart from on food labelling, advertising and a sugar tax.

This health manifesto has cherry-picked the bits that those with the loudest voices have lobbied for, for example, the cancer fund, PrEP (pre-exposure prophylaxis), sexual health and HIV services, free hospital car parking, medicines review and regulation, the children of alcoholics, young smokers, mixed sex wards and special enquiries into blood contamination and the drug Valproate. It's a jumble of ideas competing and jostling for priority. Each good intention is individually worthwhile but there's no coherence as a strategy and no connection to rights to health and social determinants of health. What is missing is the big picture of what is really happening to the NHS, social care and public health.

THE PRIVATISATION PROBLEM

Let's start with the NHS and Social Care which are considered separately:

> The next Labour government will reverse privatisation of our NHS and return our health service into expert public control. Labour will repeal the Health and Social Care Act that puts profits before patients, and make the NHS the preferred provider.

Care services have been relentlessly privatised over decades (See Pollock, 2005). The Health and Social Care (HSC) Act 2012 abolished and dismantled the NHS in England. Most social care and long-term care is delivered by for-profit companies and means-tested. Public health has been pushed out to local authorities along with many sexual health, health promotion, HIV, and children's services, and now the funding is being turned off and services closed. Long-term care has been almost completely privatised. These are structural changes. Labour's manifesto is virtually silent on the drastic and devastating system changes that have taken place as a result of the 1990 internal market and the 2012 Act. There is no whole-system approach, although the story that is being spun is one of integration of services and budgets.

> The National Care Service will be built alongside the NHS, with a shared requirement for single commissioning, partnership arrangements, pooled budgets and joint working arrangements. We will build capacity to move quickly towards a joined-up service that will signpost users to all the appropriate services at the gateway through which they arrive.

There is nothing to differentiate these aspirations from the current Conservative administration's articulation of its own policies. How exactly are sexual health, public health, mental health and children's services, which are currently so fragmented – commissioned by so many different bodies and provided by a plethora of providers – going to be reintegrated? How is long-term care provision, which is owned and operated by multinational for-profit companies, going to be integrated with publicly owned and publicly provided as well as privately operated health services? What are these partnership and joint working arrangements? How will pooled budgets and integration work, when NHS care is free and social care is charged for and means-tested? There is a marked disconnect in these aspirations.

Most worryingly is the manifesto commitment to make the NHS the preferred provider, continuing the problematic purchaser-provider split and market elements in the NHS. Is there any intention to take long-term care and social care back into public ownership and control and to have national services? Rather, the commitment is to mitigating market excesses: the manifesto declares: "We will introduce a new legal duty on the Secretary of State and on NHS England to ensure that excess private profits are not made out of the NHS at the expense of patient care."

The manifesto makes no mention of commercial contracting being virtually legally compulsory for the NHS. What are excess profits – why have profits at all? In other words, the manifesto is committed to the status quo of commercial contracting, except for limiting excess profiteering. How exactly it is going to do that is a mystery.

As for new legal duties, the primary establishing legal duty on the Secretary of State since 1946 has been to provide universal healthcare throughout. It was abolished in 2012. Why doesn't the manifesto commit the party to restoring the duty to provide, rather than saying: "We will reinstate the powers of the Secretary of State for Health to have overall responsibility for the NHS."

On the workforce, the manifesto says:

To guarantee the best possible services for patients, Labour will invest in our health and care workforce. A Labour government will step in with a long-term workforce plan for our health service that gives staff the support they need to do the best for their patients.

Once again the manifesto fails to mention the enormous deregulation of terms and conditions that has occurred as a result of commercial contracting and the internal market. NHS Foundation Trusts are structurally 49% non-NHS and can set their own terms and conditions and determine staffing levels. In the mainly private for-profit long-term care sector, most employees are low-paid women and un-unionised. This is going to get worse under current government plans for partnerships.

PARTNERSHIPS AND FRAGMENTATION

Commercial contracts and joint ventures with the private sector are at the heart of the current government's plans for radical changes to the NHS and its new models of care, termed Accountable Care Systems (ACSs) and Accountable Care Organisations (ACOs). Currently NHS England and Clinical Commissioning Groups (CCGs) are tendering for many thousands of contracts each year with multiple NHS providers and private companies bidding, all at great cost.

In future this could reduce to a few hundred contracts. The Government plans to bundle up services into giant contracts which will be awarded by CCGs and local authorities to the above-mentioned ACOs. Organisations, known variously as Multi-speciality Community Providers (MCPs) and Primary and Acute Services (PACS) comprise these private and/or public NHS providers. These large contracts will be for ten years minimum.

ACOs (MCPs and PACs) will in turn manage the risks and costs of care through subcontracts – which in turn may also sub-sub-contract for services.

NHS providers and private providers can form Special Purpose Vehicles (SPVs). According to accountants PWC, this is an

> off-balance sheet vehicle comprised of a legal entity created by the sponsor or originator, typically a major investment bank or insurance company, to fulfil a temporary objective of the sponsoring firm. SPVs can be viewed as a method of disaggregating the risks of an underlying pool of exposures held by the SPV and real-locating them to investors willing to take on those risks. This allows investors access to investment opportunities which would not otherwise exist, and provides a new source of revenue generation for the sponsoring firm.[1]

So SPVs are a mechanism for bringing in private health insurers and property companies and investment bankers. This is what integration means in the market place – bundling up services into giant contracts and tendering them out. This Labour manifesto shows no sign of distancing itself from, and abolishing the market with necessary legislation.

Labour is also committed to a new model of care:

> We will work towards a new model of community care that takes into account not only primary care but also social care and mental health. We will increase funding

to GP services to ensure patients can access the care they need. And we will halt pharmacy cuts and review provision to ensure all patients have access to pharmacy services, particularly in deprived or remote communities.

But Labour is utterly silent on how it will do this and how it will engage with the current Government's radical 'new models of care' or joint ventures, through which it is transferring risks and its responsibilities for funding and providing services to private providers and ultimately patients. The manifesto's references to partnerships and integration are ominous when there is no pledge to take back public ownership and re-nationalise the NHS and social care. GP services are being cut and increasingly run by private for profit companies.

> Labour will halt and review the NHS 'Sustainability and Transformation Plans', which are looking at closing health services across England, and ask local people to participate in the redrawing of plans with a focus on patient need rather than available finances. We will create a new quality, safety and excellence regulator – to be called 'NHS Excellence'.

Sustainability and Transformation Plans (STPs) and ACOs are the key mechanism for privatising NHS clinical services and for introducing alternative sources of funding for health care, namely health insurance and charges. Although there is as yet no legislation for STPs, ACSs and ACOs, the Government is pushing through these new organisational forms and contracts at breakneck speed, under the parliamentary radar and without public knowledge and consent, in order to bind the hands of future governments.

NHS England has already appointed clinical leads and managers to many of the 44 STPs, and has spent over £20m on management consultants and staff.[2] For example, a contract worth £2.7m has been awarded to Capita by Nottinghamshire and Nottingham STP to support the area's sustainability developments. Capita in turn has subcontracted with Centene UK, an American insurance company, to provide expertise and run its STP as it moves to ACS status.[3] Centene's core business in the US is in the Medicaid Managed Care market, whereby private insurers control government budgets for the poor, contract with providers, and pocket the difference. Following some highly profitable acquisitions in the US, the company announced its intentions to expand abroad and already has a partnership arrangement with the Valencia government's corporate partner in the Alzira health service, Ribera Salud. Ribera Salud is currently under police investigation for corruption.[4]

It's also been recently announced that Nottingham CCG has tendered a contract for community services worth £205m as part of the intended ACS. Given those now involved in the ACS formation, it can safely be assumed this will be awarded to a private company. At least eight other STPs are reported to be following suit in developing ACSs, and will receive £450m of transformation funding from NHS England.

Halting and reviewing STPs is a first step but it won't go far enough: the changes are being driven by NHS England. The Labour manifesto is silent on the fact that most Foundation Trusts (FTs), which since 2012 have had new powers to enter into joint ventures and to generate 49% of their income from private patients and other non-NHS sources, are entering into giant contracts of their own with property management companies.

On funding,

> Labour will boost capital funding for the NHS, to ensure that patients are cared for in buildings and using equipment that are fit for the 21st century. And we will introduce a new Office for Budget Responsibility for Health to oversee health spending and scrutinise how it is spent.

But there is no mention in the manifesto of the crippling costs of the Private Finance Initiative (PFI). A recent study by the Centre for Health and the Public Interest calculated that £831m had been made in pre-tax profits by PFI companies over the past six years, money which has not been available for patient care. This figure is equivalent to at least a quarter of the total NHS hospital deficit over the same period.[5]

The Department of Health's annual capital budget has been frozen in cash terms over the five years to 2020-21. Much of its revenue funding has been rebadged as capital, for example, relabelled Research and Development revenue funding, depreciation and previously committed expenditure. Moreover it is being used to balance growing revenue deficits in the NHS Trust sector. In 2016-17 the DH Annual report and accounts reported that £1.2 billion of capital was moved to revenue expenditure in that year, a recurring pattern year on year.[6]

To get around the lack of capital as well as the affordability, debt and deficit problems, FTs, especially those with PFI and deficits, are entering into various forms of joint venture in order to transform estate ownership and control. A hospital trust entering into an SPV with the clinical services income attached will have the additional attraction of being able to generate income from such services to pay the heavy debt charges and to raise borrowings for new capital using existing NHS property and to refinance PFI schemes.

University College Birmingham NHS FT has, for example, recently linked up with the Healthcare Corporation of America (HCA) to build a mixed economy facility of 72 public and 66 private beds. According to the Trust, all capital has been provided by HCA. As an FT it can generate up to half its income privately. As such it is well positioned to become an ACO model. HCA currently has four joint ventures with NHS hospitals, including University College Hospital London and the Christie in Manchester.[7]

Another form of joint venture, is the Strategic Estate Partnership (SEP). These 55 partnerships between the public and private sectors are intended to give the former greater control through non-exclusive contractual relationships where different stages of the process will be open to renewed tendering. In theory at least, this will mean a continual appraisal of value for money arrangements. In practice, however, SEPs are largely about maximising revenue creation in as many ways as possible, including developing retail outlets, car parking, patient hotels, sales and disposals, and private patient units.[8] Indeed many former PFI companies, such as Interserve, Prime and the Rydon Group, have simply transferred their attention to this new model which, given the scale of investment opportunities involved, could be considered a type of 'PFI Plus'.

There are currently more than eight SEPs reported on commercial and contracting websites, though it is hard to find any detail on Department of Health and NHS websites. The first SEP was at Lancashire Care Foundation Trust, with others now including Cheshire and Wirral Partnership FT, University Hospital Southampton FT, Isle of Wight Trust, Yeovil District Hospital FT and one at Hinchingbrooke following the collapse of Circle's management of the Trust. Several more are in the pipeline. These include North West Anglia NHS FT, Oxleas NHS FT, and Whittington Hospital NHS Trust.

The manifesto does not mention the selling off of NHS assets to create revenue for the Treasury. Yet a key attraction of joint ventures, which allow investment bankers and property management companies to partner in health care, is the sale and disposal of NHS assets. Since the HSC Act 2012, the Government has paved the way for privatisation of non-FT estate with the abolition of NHS Estates and creation of two Department of Health-wholly owned companies, NHS Property Services and

Community Health Partnerships. NHS Property Services holds the estate of Primary Care Trusts and Strategic Health Authorities which was not transferred to trusts and is among the largest property owners in Europe. It is now charging exorbitant market rents to the NHS and GPs, to such an extent that small GP practices are closing and trusts and CCGs are struggling to pay. Community Health Partnerships include 49 Local Improvement Financial Trust Companies with investment of £2.5 billion and 339 facilities involving 29 companies.

NHS England has created six regional public-private partnerships to help speed up disposals, and once approval has been obtained, these will be advertised in the *Official Journal of the European Union* in six lots worth more than £3bn. Codenamed Project Phoenix, "private companies will work with the NHS to achieve the best market price for the sales without the requirement of upfront public investment, with profits shared between the NHS and its private partners. Details of the profit split have yet to be revealed", according to the *Health Service Journal*.[9] In August this year Primary Health Properties, Octopus Healthcare and Assura came forward with a combined offer of £3.3bn of investment, which they say would provide the entire private capital necessary to embed STP plans and fund up to 750 new primary care centres at an approximate rental value of £200m per annum. All three companies incorporate both investment and property arms and are based offshore.[10] According to a LaingBuisson market report on primary care from 2015, the three companies, at a combined aggregate of £2.27bn, already had a 19% share of the estimated asset value of all GP premises in the UK.[11] Harry Hyman, managing director of Primary Health Properties, has been quick to say that this is not a form of PFI, rather a "continuation of our business model where we own the properties and rent them for the period of the lease."[12]

The manifesto makes four pledges for increasing funding:

We will increase the social care budgets by a further £8 billion over the lifetime of the next Parliament, including an additional £1 billion for the first year. This will be enough for providers to pay a real living wage...Labour will commit to over £30 billion in extra funding over the next Parliament through increasing income tax for the highest 5 per cent of earners and by increasing tax on private medical insurance, and we will free up resources by halving the fees paid to management consultants.

Of course more funding is necessary. By 2015–16, NHS commissioners, NHS trusts and NHS FTs reported a combined deficit of £1.85 billion, a greater than threefold increase in the deficit position of £574 million reported in 2014–15. Provider trusts' overall deficit grew by 185% to £2.45 billion, up from £859 million in 2014–15, against a total income of £75.97 billion.

In addition, two-thirds of NHS trusts (65%) and NHS FTs (66%) reported deficits in 2015-16, up from 44% of NHS trusts and 51% of NHS FTs in the previous financial year. The number of CCGs reporting cumulative deficits was 32 in 2015–16, up from 19 in both 2014–15 and 2013–14.[13]

However, the Labour manifesto fails to address where the money is going, namely the transactions costs of the market (12-30%), the high costs of PFI and prices of drugs and technologies which rise ahead of NHS pay and the costs of management consultants. It is silent on the enormous costs of administering a market, a market which it plans to retain, stating only that it will free up resources by halving the fees paid to management consultants.

THE NHS REINSTATEMENT BILL

Most surprisingly, the manifesto makes no mention of what will replace the HSC Act 2012 and no mention of the NHS Reinstatement Bill, which Jeremy Corbyn and John McDonnell supported before becoming leader and shadow chancellor respectively. This Bill has been tabled three times in the House of Commons, most recently by Margaret Greenwood MP.

The next Labour manifesto must now remedy the catastrophe that is unravelling and commit to the NHS Reinstatement Bill.[14] Unless this happens, there will be no NHS.

The Bill proposes to fully restore the NHS as an accountable public service by reversing 25 years of marketisation in the NHS, abolishing the purchaser-provider split, ending contracting and re-establishing public bodies and public services accountable to local communities. This is necessary to stop the dismantling of the NHS under the HSC Act 2012. It is driven by the needs of

local communities. Scotland and Wales have already reversed
marketisation and restored their NHS without massive upheaval.
England can too.

The Bill provides flexibility in how it would be implemented,
led by local authorities and current bodies. It would:

- reinstate the Government's duty to provide the key
  NHS services throughout England, including hospitals, medical and nursing services, primary care,
  mental health and community services;
- integrate health and social care services;
- declare the NHS to be a "non-economic service of
  general interest" and "a service supplied in the exercise of governmental authority," so asserting the full
  competence of Parliament and the devolved bodies
  to legislate for the NHS without being trumped by
  EU competition law and the World Trade Organi-
  zation's General Agreement on Trade in Services;
- abolish the NHS Commissioning Board (NHS
  England) and re-establish it as a Special Health
  Authority with regional committees;
- plan and provide services without contracts
  through Health Boards, which could cover more
  than one local authority area if there was local
  support;
- allow local authorities to lead a 'bottom up' process
  with the assistance of CCGs, NHS trusts, NHS FTs

and NHS England to transfer, functions to Health Boards;

- abolish NHS trusts, NHS foundation trusts and CCGs after the transfer;

- abolish Monitor – the regulator of NHS FTs, commercial companies and voluntary organisations – and repeal the competition and core marketsation provisions of the 2012 Act;

- integrate public health services and the duty to reduce inequalities, into the NHS;

- re-establish Community Health Councils to represent the interest of the public in the NHS;

- stop licence conditions taking effect which have been imposed by Monitor on NHS foundation trusts and which reduce the number of services they currently have to provide;

- introduce a system for collective bargaining across the NHS;

- centralise NHS debts under the PFI in the Treasury, require publication of PFI contracts and also require the Treasury to report to Parliament on reducing NHS PFI debts;

- abolish the legal provisions passed in 2014 requiring certain immigrants to pay for NHS services;

- declare the UK's agreement to the proposed Transatlantic Trade and Investment Partnership and other international treaties affecting the NHS to

require the prior approval of Parliament and the
devolved legislatures;

- require the Government to report annually to Parliament on the effect of treaties on the NHS.

CONCLUSION

By 2011 David Bennett the former head of Monitor, the economic regulator of the NHS, was telling the *Times*: "The NHS is ripe
for dismemberment."[15] He declared to the House of Commons
health select committee: "We, in the UK, have done this in other
sectors before. We did it in gas, we did it in power, we did it in
telecoms… We've done it in rail, we've done it in water, so there's
actually 20 years of experience in taking monopolistic, monolith-
ic markets and providers and exposing them to economic regulation."[16]

On September 27th 2016, Diane Abbott, then shadow health
secretary, stated at the Labour Party conference stated:

Under Jeremy Corbyn's leadership, the Labour Party
will be committed to halting and reversing the tide of
privatisation and marketisation of the NHS. The Health
and Social Care Act has fragmented the system, making
it so much easier for the private sector to move in. Conference, Labour in government will repeal the Health
and Social Care Act. This means returning our NHS to

what is was originally conceived as: a publicly owned, publicly funded, publicly accountable universal service as outlined in the NHS Reinstatement Bill now being expertly piloted through Parliament by my colleague Margaret Greenwood, MP for Wirral West, with the support of the Labour leadership.[17]

We must all hold the Labour Party to that pledge.

The author wishes to acknowledge the help of Stewart Player for his contribution to the analysis of NHS estates.

REFERENCES

Pollock, Allyson M, *NHS PLC: The privatisation of our health care* (Verso, 2005).

8. SAFER COMMUNITIES

Chris Williamson

MANIFESTO SUMMARY

Labour will support the police in the performance of their duties, ensuring there are enough officers, support staff and equipment to protect our communities, including from the growing threat of cybercrime. Working with Police and Crime Commissioners throughout the country, we will champion community policing and incentivise best practice, eliminating institutional biases against BAME communities. We will recruit 10,000 more community police officers and introduce statutory minimum standards for services from criminal justice agencies. Labour will appoint a commissioner to set new standards for tackling domestic and sexual violence, establish a National Refuge Fund to ensure stability for rape crisis centres, make relationship and sex education a compulsory part of the curriculum and strengthen the law on domestic violence.

On counter-terrorism, Labour will maintain cross-border security cooperation with our partners in Europe and beyond. Judicial oversight will be reintroduced over investigatory powers and the Prevent programme will be reviewed, to address the Government's failure to take effective new measures against extreme radicalisation.

On border security, while the Conservatives cut the Border Force and sought to turn landlords, teachers and medical staff into unpaid immigration officials, Labour will recruit 500 more border guards to improve our safeguards.

Labour will halt cuts to the fire service and recruit 3,000 new firefighters, reinstating separate governance for the Fire and Police Services. Fire and Rescue Services will have a statutory duty to coordinate and respond to floods.

Labour will retain the Human Rights Act and hold public inquiries into historic injustices, including Orgreave and blacklisting. We will release all papers relating to the Shrewsbury 24 trials and Cammell Laird ship workers. We will review the appointments process to make the judiciary more representative. We will immediately re-establish early advice entitlements in the Family Courts and end the requirement for victims of domestic abuse to have to pay to have their injuries certificated. We will legislate to stop the cross-examination of victims by their abuser in some circumstances. Funding for the preparation of judicial review cases will be reintroduced and legal aid mean tests reviewed. Labour will introduce no-fault divorce and consult on creating an environmental tribunal to simplify legal challenges to government in this field.

To tackle overcrowding in prisons, Labour will publish annual reports on prisoner-staff ratios. Lifting the public sector pay cap will help recruitment and retention and there will be no fur-ther privatisation. To tackle re-offending, Labour will demand personal rehabilitation plans for all prisoners, as well as review-ing mental health services in prisons. We will build on our record of innovative models of youth justice and, in the context of the failure of the part-privatisation of Probation Services, we will re-view the role of Community Rehabilitation Companies.

***

Justice is all too often denied. Too many ordinary peo-ple know this. There are football fans, trade unionists, environmental activists and people living with disabil-ities whose personal experiences provide first-hand testimony.

– Labour's 2017 manifesto.

It wasn't simply the tabloid press that misjudged Corbyn's chanc-es in June. The election result showed that the vast rump of Britain's commentariat were also dramatically wrong-footed in their prediction that Labour's manifesto would fail to resonate with voters. In an editorial on 15th May, soon after the manifesto had been leaked to the press, *The Guardian* wrote that "Labour's agenda has the appearance of a backward-looking union special interest wish-list, not the overarching response to the new world of work the country needs."

But who was really backward-looking? Was it the electorate who, not for the first time, had voted for something that struck fear into the heart of liberal commentators, or was it the latter, whose own superior insight marked their distance from the experiences of ordinary people?

Those normal experiences and their relevance to Labour's manifesto are the focus of this chapter. I want to show how things changed immensely in the twenty years since Tony Blair won a landslide for Labour in 1997. But while life moved on, the commentariat failed to keep up.

For them, the election of Jeremy Corbyn as Labour leader represented merely an unwelcome echo of the 1970s. They simply refused to engage with the hundreds of thousands who joined Labour to support Jeremy, preferring to bury their heads in the sand of an immutable neoliberal consensus. Britain's big media and political classes patronisingly attributed the dramatic 2015 Labour leadership election to the actions of a mindless herd of posttruthers dancing to the tune of a dangerous group of Trotskyites.

But then Brexit happened. The disbelief in the newsrooms and restaurants around Westminster went into overdrive. The same question was being asked everywhere: "Who is out of touch here: us, or them?"

In one effort to find an answer *The Guardian* dispatched John Harris on a tour of Britain's lesser-known provinces to meet the natives. His video series reported back to *Guardian* readers a sense of their problem: that the experiences of many ordinary people stubbornly refused to match the paper's political views. Yet despite this, Harris and company stubbornly refused to change their impression of the Labour leader and the Party's recent left turn.

In an article published in March 2017, Harris asked whether anyone could rescue Labour from its deep irrelevance. He opined that despite recognising "a lot of people voted to leave the EU because of the chance to alert the political establishment to problems that had for too long been ignored," Corbyn, a life-long anti-establishment figure with a radical agenda, was instructed by Harris to "be on his way".[1]

Inside the Labour Party, this chatter resulted in the critique that Corbyn had failed to halt the tide of post-truth irrationality, exemplified by the EU referendum result. The unimaginative prescription proposed was a return to centrist realism as the only possible dam that could contain Britain's popular extremes. The fact that the same strategy had been failing for Labour since 2010, with the decline beginning much earlier, did not matter.

From different quarters, and taking their cues from Nigel Farage, a second tendency in the Party claimed Labour had lost touch with the working class, who were anti-internationalist, typically white and uninterested in Corbyn's metropolitan brand of socialism. These were the authentic constituents Labour was relinquishing: that multitude of weary workers, fearful of croissants, Belgium and all forms of difference. This second group did recognise the anti-establishment mood of the electorate yet was ready to abandon our Party's commitment to socialism in the same spirit as Oswald Mosley.

Within this deafening confusion, the only plausible third way was Corbynism, offering a radical alternative that was both pitch perfect with the times and left wing.

None of this prehistory matters now. It simply highlights the mismatch between two realities, one depicted by the bulk of Britain's politicians and pundits and another as it is for ordinary people over the past three decades. I also recount this narrative to help come to terms with the two years of chatter that, as George Orwell wrote in *1984*, "penetrated inside your skull, battering against your brain, frightening you out of your beliefs, persuading you, almost, to deny the evidence of your senses." Corbyn supporters can have the confidence to state with certainty that two plus two does not equal five, as many commentators before 8th June had suggested.

AUSTERITY REJECTED

Labour's 2017 manifesto expresses what I like to call common sense socialism. The ideas in those pages are not evergreen ideological claptrap, a defence of moderation in immoderate times, neither do they fuel a fire of division. Labour's commitments capture the spirit of the nation as it actually is. The manifesto is a rejection of the ideological commitment to austerity, cast in the terms of "realism" and "centrism". It is popular, simply because for the vast majority of voters who have lived in the age of no alternatives, needless wars, inequality and austerity, it frames the status quo as a form of extremism.

Labour has at its disposal an insurgent socialist common sense. That common sense is shaped by our Party's ideas that resonate with popular experiences. Some examples, drawn from the campaign and immediately after, illustrate this.

Not long after launching my campaign to win back the seat of Derby North, which I lost in 2015 by a mere 41 votes, one constituent I met requested my help with an issue. The constituent had been the victim of a credit consolidation scam run by a now defunct firm called Compass Debt Counsellors. Compass, it turned out, was owned and run by the husband of the Tory MP for Derby North, who was my opponent in the election. A member of my team did a little digging and found a victim support group on Facebook for those who had lost money through Compass. There were over 80 people in the group, each having lost amounts ranging from £5,000 to £25,000. A liquidation report acquired through the group revealed that 1,700 of the firm's clients had lost a total of £5.5 million at the hands of this company.

The firm took advantage of weak regulation and even weaker enforcement that permitted Compass to quite simply rob its clients. This rogue company offered those suffering the burden of private debt to collect regular repayments, which they said would be saved in order to build up a pot in order to negotiate a reduced settlement with the original creditors – a realistic aim and common practice, but one which never materialised. Prior to folding, Compass' shareholders repeatedly paid themselves huge dividends from the pot of their client's money. Millions were paid into Compass by vulnerable clients trying to do the right thing but next to nothing was left by the time the scam ended.

Like the constituent I met during the campaign, all the victims had been abandoned by the state thrice over. First, in the sense in which the management of our economy creates conditions of precarity that will inevitably lead towards a dependence on private debt, a problem that has not gone away, as private debt today hovers dangerously close to its pre-financial crash total. Second, lax regulation and enforcement standards in all aspects of society, including finance, have been a significant feature of every government since 1979, which have adopted a so-called 'business-friendly' and 'anti-red tape' agenda. And third, the Financial Conduct Authority's decision to spurn the people who have been ripped off by the avaricious directors of Compass by refusing to bring the victims within the scope of the FCA's compensation scheme. This last point remains an essential demand of the Compass Debt Campaign that I have since helped to establish.

The net result of this experience, for the 1,700 plus victims and their families, is the sense that there is little justice in our society. Are they right? Could having recently witnessed the biggest bailout of private banks in history and experienced the resulting austerity have left a mark in their minds, or are their complaints of injustice simply more 'post-truth' irrationality?

SAFER COMMUNITIES

A significant event during the campaign was the bombing at the Manchester Arena. As news rolled in of the terror attack, of the dead and injured children, I was glued to my television all night. I stayed pretty much in a state of disbelief and mourning well into the next day. Once talk resumed of when the election campaign would begin again, a view emerged among the chattering classes that the attack would spell the end for Corbyn. Labour had come a long way in the opinion polls but, everyone claimed that Corbyn was bad on the issue of national security.

Not so. Despite the mainstream media narrative, Corbyn addressed a nation that was in a state of shock and grief, but one that also harboured the memories of needless war and intervention that have destabilised the region from which the bulk of terror flowed. The Labour leader spoke to people in the same way as the victims of Compass wanted to be addressed: he validated their experiences, without being 'moderate', yet without a trace of the politics of division. Had the Iraq war achieved its aim of stabilising Iraq? No. British people had died and it had very much made things worse. A bombing campaign in Libya and an unwillingness to clean up the mess there had also created chaos in the very country in which the Manchester bomber, Salman Abedi, had trained.

Corbyn spelled out the simple fact that cuts to Britain's police force undermined our security, particularly as the nature of criminal activities has shifted. There is increasing online crime such as fraud[2] and child sexual exploitation, which have been widely reported in recent years. This cybercrime phenomenon was unimaginable in the 1980s and poses new challenges for modern policing and policymakers, yet the Tories response has been to cut 20,000 frontline police officers.

The Conservatives cite the Crime Survey, which shows a steady decline since the 1980s in crimes like murder, robberies, gun and knife crime and household burglaries. But the one constant is that working-class communities are hardest hit by crime. Research by the Joseph Rowntree Foundation confirmed that people living in poor neighbourhoods are generally more likely to be the victims and/or perpetrators of crime.[3] This feeds the demonisation of poorer communities by certain sections of the media, which was highlighted by Owen Jones in his 2011 book *Chavs* (Verso, 2011).

The governance of the Police Service has also seen a radical shift with the introduction of Police and Crime Commissioners. Neighbourhood Policing Teams, sometimes referred to as Safer Neighbourhood Teams, were embedded in local communities and Police and Community Support Officers were introduced in 2002. Yet, despite these changes, fear of crime still outstrips actual crime. Moreover, the investment in the policing service by the last Labour Government has been slashed. Ever since the Conservatives came to power in 2010, funding for policing has been reduced.

Community policing is now in very real jeopardy, particularly as resources are needed to tackle the new threats from cybercrime and terrorism. Pressure is mounting to extend privatisation to cover policing just as in nearly every other area of public service.

David Cameron once described the police as "the last great unreformed public service".[4] He was a special advisor to John

Major's Government which commissioned the Sheehy Review in 1993. That review marked an earlier attempt by the Conservatives to subject the police to market principles.

The relentless austerity programme, started by George Osborne in 2010, is being used as a convenient fig leaf to facilitate privatisation of whole swathes of our public services, and the Police Service is no exception. Privateers like G4S, Capita and Serco are circling like vultures waiting to enjoy the rich pickings from the bones of local constabularies across the country.

We've already seen Lincolnshire awarding a lucrative contract to G4S, and Oliver Letwin, who was previously the minister responsible for co-ordinating government policy, has publicly stated his support for private sector involvement in the Police Service. Letwin says this shouldn't even be a matter of political debate, rather a "straightforward and obvious…way of conducting business in this country".[5]

But despite the Conservative Party's obsession with shrinking the state and using public services as a cash cow for privateers, they have failed to convince the electorate, for whom privatisation is very far from being an obvious way of conducting business.

The Conservative Party's preoccupation with cuts and privatisation exposes their Achilles' heel on crime and disorder. There is no public appetite for this Tory obsession, which is why people are increasingly looking to Labour to protect communities, thanks to the Party's unambiguous commitment to increase police numbers and reverse the privatisation agenda.

Going forward, Labour has the public's attention on this issue, which will enable us to make the case for a more progressive approach to crime and policing, which includes offering people the opportunity to be part of the solution. Momentum and local Constituency Labour Parties could harness the mass movement to help facilitate a debate on a range of issues affecting crime and policing, which impinge on the quality of life in urban and rural communities alike. Such a bottom-up approach is precisely what Jeremy Corbyn spoke about in his successful leadership campaigns and it is this approach which underpinned the 2017 manifesto.

The tentacles of the privatisation agenda have turned the criminal justice system into a giant money-making racket for the same privateers who are eyeing up new ways to make money out of our police service.

But Labour offers an alternative. The manifesto acknowledges that budget cuts and privatisation have eroded justice for the many – now increasingly the preserve of the few – and therefore commits Labour to looking at ways of reinstating access to justice. One way this could be facilitated is by devolving funding for the criminal justice system to local areas. This would provide an impetus for greater collaboration, sustainable solutions and more opportunities to involve the public in restorative justice options, which the manifesto pledges to embed across all youth offending institutions.

The present system is broken. Involving the private sector, which is driven by the profit motive, can result in perverse incentives. For example, increases in the prison population generate additional funding streams, which maximises profits and dividends for shareholders. Where is the incentive to rehabilitate offenders or identify community solutions?

It is little surprise that the involvement of the private sector over the last 30 years has coincided with an exponential rise in the prison population. England and Wales have the highest per capita prison population in western Europe – 147 people per 100,000 and Scotland has the second highest at 143 per 100,000.[6]

The costs of sending someone to prison are colossal. For a young offender it is more than £87,000 per year.[7] But the costs of locking up children and adolescents in secure children's homes and secure training centres are substantially greater. The cost per young person in a secure training centre is around £170,000 per annum and for secure children's homes around £210,000.[8] – even higher in certain circumstances. Yet despite these enormous sums, these institutions are catastrophically failing the young people in their care. The re-offending rate is around 70%.

When the Government is spending almost six times more than it costs to send a child to Eton[9], yet the system is still disastrously failing these young people, it is time for a radical rethink. The almost £3 billion spent every year on incarcerating people in England and Wales could be deployed much more effectively.

The first step should be to remove the profit motive by overturning the privatisations that have seen prisons and 70% of the probation service sold to the private sector. The manifesto pledge to review the role of Community Rehabilitation Companies is therefore essential.

Jettisoning the business model, and the culture of 'payment by results', would also have a beneficial impact because they can lead to perverse outcomes, particularly when private sector organisations are involved. The Government's 'Troubled Families' initiative is a case in point. Local authorities were asked to identify families who "cause high costs to the taxpayer." In addition two out of these three categories then needed to apply:

- Youth crime or anti-social behaviour;
- Children who are regularly truanting or not in school;
- An adult on out of work benefits.[10]

The payment by results regime meant that measurable improvements had to be achieved. The grand claims that have subsequently been made about the success of this programme have been met with derision in many quarters.[11]

But the supreme perverse outcome is that the most troubled families were not touched by this project because of concerns about the difficulties in obtaining the results and thereby the payments. Consequently, some of the families in greatest need of support have not received any under this scheme.

The proposal contained in the manifesto to "incentivise local authorities, police forces and probation services to engage effectively with young people at risk of drifting into anti-social or criminal behaviours" would help to redress the failed system that is currently in place. If this were developed to include devolving the criminal justice budget to local authorities, it would create an incentive to secure better outcomes, without the need to dance to the latest Whitehall whim. Bottom-up solutions like this are invariably better and more sustainable.

If more were invested in preventing people getting entangled in the criminal justice system by deterring crime through initiatives like targeted youth work and providing better life chances, as envisaged in Labour's manifesto, far fewer people would find themselves on the wrong side of the law. This would not only be a better use of public money, it would also reduce the number of people whose lives are ruined by criminal behaviour – both victims and perpetrators alike.

Border security is yet another area where the Conservative Party's obsession with neoliberal ideology has had a negative effect on service delivery. As the manifesto makes clear, this is a vital area in terms of "preventing serious crimes including child abduction, people trafficking, smuggling of drugs and guns, terrorism and modern day slavery."

Border security should not be a licence to print money for the private sector. Yet that is precisely what is happening with public money being used to generate private profit rather than deliver a public service, even in this sensitive area.[12]

Labour's plan to recruit 500 more public sector border guards would help to deal with the malaise that has afflicted border security as a result of years of underinvestment and privatisation. A reinvigorated public sector border security service, as proposed in the manifesto, working in conjunction with rejuvenated police forces, would help to keep Britain safer.

AFTER GRENFELL

Finally, to turn to an experience that, like the Manchester attack, will haunt the political consciousness of the nation for decades to come. The fire at Grenfell took the lives of more than 80, mostly BAME, working class people who literally burnt to death in their own homes. The immediate response of the local working class community was anger: the fire confirmed their previous experiences of dealing with the local authority and government. Indeed, one community group had repeatedly warned of the danger. In a blog post from November 2016, Grenfell Action Group wrote "only a catastrophic event will expose the ineptitude and incompetence of our landlord, the KCTMO [Kensington & Chelsea Tenant Management Organisation], and bring an end to the dangerous living conditions and neglect of health and safety legislation that they inflict upon their tenants and leaseholders."[13]

It wasn't the first time a tower block fire had had deadly consequences. In 2009, six people died in a fire at Lakanal House in South London. A coroner's report recommended that the relevant building regulations be examined and updated, which the Conservative Minister for Housing, Gavin Barwell, finally promised to do in 2015, but only after persistent pressure from campaigners. However, the review failed to materialise. The fact that Barwell's promise amounted to nothing is unsurprising, in view of the Government's approach to new regulation, which has been 'one in, one out' (whereby for every new regulation imposed, an old one must be scrapped), in a bid to make all aspects of public life more profitable for the private sector.

Grenfell goes to the heart of successive governments' wilful ignorance of public safety concerns. Since Thatcher, competition has been introduced in all aspects of public life. The privatisation of building inspectors eroded the quality of inspections as costs were lowered in order to compete. It also created incentives for inspectors to strike a permissible attitude with their clients, namely the developers. The Thatcherite anti-state obsession has likewise seen publicly funded inspectors cut, along with 11,000 frontline firefighters in the past seven years. The Blair Government's decision to transfer responsibility for determining the fire safety of buildings, from the Fire and Rescue Service to the owners, was meant to be another blow against what neoliberals pejoratively term the 'nanny state'.

Should we be labelling those who are angered by the Grenfell fire as 'post-truthers'? Should it be our job to lower the expectations of campaigners and put the marker for justice far below what is needed? Should we explain to the families of the dead that our moderate realist ideology, rooted in Thatcherism, requires that we cannot reverse cuts to fire inspectors and firefighters, nor properly regulate the construction industry? The thought is absurd. Politics today requires radical answers because people are increasingly recognising that they live in radical times.

To return to the epigraph to this chapter, justice is repeatedly denied to ordinary people – from the private debtor negotiating a rigged economy composed of so many crony capitalists, to the victims and survivors of a terror campaign that has been fuelled by the chaos of western intervention. They, along with all those who witnessed Grenfell, share experiences that create a popular common sense that will eventually drive Labour's proposals into government. Our testimony, the testimony of the people, is the fabric of the Labour Party's socialism. Recognising that is how we will win the next election and set about creating a new consensus that will consign neoliberal brutality to history and herald an era of common sense socialist hegemony.

9. LEADING RICHER LIVES

Jeremy Gilbert

MANIFESTO SUMMARY

Labour believes in devolving power to local communities, including over economic development, and giving them the necessary funding to do the job. We will give local government extra funding next year, conduct a review into reforming council tax and business rates and look at new options like a land value tax. Labour will give new powers to planning authorities enabling them to put communities at the heart of planning and updating compulsory purchase orders to drive regeneration. We will end the cuts to youth services, support all training routes for social workers, prevent the private sector from running child protection services and improve protection for victims of abuse by strengthening mandatory reporting. To promote the care of vulnerable children, we will support further regulation of commercial fostering agencies and look at establishing a national fostering service. We will extend arrangements to support young people in care until age 21, enshrine the UN Convention on the Rights of the Child into domestic law and scrap child burial fees. Labour will reintroduce library standards, end the closure of post offices and look at establishing a Post Bank. Communities will be given more power to shape their town centres and protect key facilities with a national review of local pubs to examine their demise. Labour will regulate and greatly reduce the maximum stake on Fixed Odds Betting Terminals. We will give members of the Local Government Pension Scheme full trustee status. For rural areas, Labour will invest in housing, transport, broadband, coastal protection and flood management and introduce a process where all policies consider their impact on rural communities. To prioritise tourism, we will reinstate the cross-Whitehall ministerial group on tourism. We will expand the role of the Groceries Code Adjudicator, reconfigure funds for farming and fishing to support smaller traders, allow EU workers employed in these fields to stay in the UK and reinstate the Seasonal Agricultural Workers Scheme and the Agricultural Wages Board. We will make utility companies return roads to a condition no worse than they found them.

Labour will bring our railways back into public ownership as franchises expire. We will cap fares, introduce free wifi, ensure safe staffing levels and improve disability access. New rolling stock will be publicly owned and we will encourage the expansion of public freight services. As stated elsewhere, we will complete HS2, build a Crossrail of the North and other projects, delivering nationwide rail electrification and consulting on reopening branch lines. We will extend the powers to re-regulate local bus services and support the creation of municipal bus companies.

Routes of critical community value will be protected. We will retrofit thousands of diesel buses in areas with the most severe air quality problems to Euro 6 standards and introduce national standards for taxis and hire cars. We will upgrade the National Cycle Network and our highways, improve roadworks at known bottlenecks and scrap the Severn Bridge tolls. We will guarantee that any airport expansion in the South East adheres to strict environmental criteria. We will look at port development, invest in the devolved regions and continue working with EU transport institutions.

We will extend environmental protection and champion sustainable farming and fishing. We will give the Fire and Rescue Services a statutory duty to co-ordinate and respond to floods. Labour will introduce a Clean Air Act, safeguard marine habitats and set targets for plastic waste reduction. We will take measures to protect bees and plant a million native trees. Forests will be kept in public hands and a science innovation fund established.

Labour will increase the maximum sentence for animal cruelty offences, promote cruelty-free animal husbandry, prohibit the third party sale of puppies, cease the badger cull and ban ivory trading and wild animals in circuses.

Labour will introduce a £1 billion Cultural Capital Fund, administered by the Arts Council over a five year period. We will invest in museums, maintaining free entry, supporting local arts provision, and widening the reach of the Government Art Collection. Labour will introduce an arts pupil premium in every primary school in England – £160 million a year. We will put creativity back into the curriculum, reviewing the Ebacc performance measure to ensure arts are not sidelined. Labour will launch a creative careers advice campaign in schools and work with employers and unions to agree guidelines on pay and standards in the performing arts. We will work with broadcasters and the film industry to improve diversity and with all sides in digital industries to improve rewards for innovators. Labour will review extending the £1,000 pub relief business rates scheme to small music venues and change planning law to ensure they can coexist with new housing developments. Labour will ensure tech companies take measures to protect children from online abuse.

Labour is committed to keeping Channel 4 in public ownership and will guarantee the future of Welsh-language broadcaster S4C. On phone hacking, Labour will implement the recommendations of part one of the Leveson Enquiry and initiate part two, looking into corporate governance failure. We will review plurality in local media ownership and strengthen Ofcom in this area.

In sport, we will give football supporters greater say in how clubs are run, legislating for accredited supporters trusts to be able to appoint and remove at least two club directors and to purchase shares. We will improve disability access to sports fixtures and ensure the Premier League deliver on its promise to invest 5% of its TV rights income into the grassroots game. Labour will improve opportunities for fans to have fair access to tickets.

***

There's no question that Labour's June 2017 General Election manifesto marked a historic turning point, because of its symbolic break with many years of neoliberal orthodoxy. However, *Leading Richer Lives* is not its most coherent section. Ranging from local government to arts and media policy, it's unclear why this particular range of politics was grouped together, apart from the fact that the authors didn't know where else to put them. This sense of randomness, along with the section's vague title, suggests that this was a document put together almost exclusively by economists, with little sense of how any other area of public policy might fit into a broad and coherent political vision.

That's not to say that any of its proposals are bad, or that they have nothing to do with each other. But most of them could have been dealt with under other headings, and in places they seem to betray very little effort to think beyond the limits of established neoliberal assumptions. However, my purpose here is not primarily to criticise the manifesto, but to suggest ways in which its welcome intentions could be carried forward, informed by a radical analysis of the problems which it seeks to address.

One key point to make is this. Much of what I will argue here amounts to pointing out that a lot of the manifesto (or at least this section) was not really very radical. However, it is important to note that Labour's stunning election success in June 2017 was achieved on the basis of the widespread belief that the manifesto was extremely radical, with its most left-wing policies being those which received by far the most publicity. Nobody voted Labour because they liked the moderate and unchallenging tone of many of the sections of the manifesto that I am about to criticise (which, without doubt, almost no voters actually read).

Therefore, these criticisms should be read as constructive in nature, and fully in tune with the spirit of the Corbyn agenda. Their purpose is to help our party and our movement develop a programme which is as genuinely progressive as most of the electorate already assume that it is.

LOCAL COMMUNITIES: DEVOLUTION OR EMPOWERMENT?

"Labour believes in devolving power to local communities", the manifesto says: an admirable sentiment. The trouble is, so does everyone. No manifesto from any party, for many years, has not promised to devolve power to local communities, in one form or another. What marks this as a new and important set of proposals is the statement which follows: "but that requires the necessary funding follows. You cannot empower local government if you impoverish it". This is an excellent departure, but it ultimately offers to address only a part of the problem facing local democracy in the UK today. In acknowledging that power follows from resourcing, the manifesto makes a radical step. At the same time, however, the framing of the issue here rehearses one of the most problematic canards of British political discourse – the idea that central government has simply accrued power to itself, which it is now able to 'devolve' to localities if it so wishes.

But this simply isn't what's happened to local government since the 1970s. It would be far more accurate to say that central government has overseen a series of transfers of power from public bodies at all levels – especially, but not exclusively, local government – to the private sector. It isn't central government that now holds the power that once resided with local authorities: it's property developers and huge financial firms such as PricewaterhouseCoopers. The issue therefore is not simply one of central government handing out power to local authorities, but of rebuilding local communities and their institutions as alternative loci of real social power, capable of challenging the influence of finance capital and its own local agents. While the manifesto promises legislation to strengthen and democratise the local planning process, it nonetheless makes no significant proposals for actually mobilising local communities as democratic social forces, particularly in the face of the obvious political resistance that any such legislative efforts would provoke.

The question then is: what kind of policies could actually facilitate such a process? One much-touted policy in recent years has been the programme of 'participatory budgeting' pioneered in the Brazilian city of Porto Alegre in the 1990s. This involves municipal budgets being determined by a process of rolling neighbourhood meetings, delegating to similar rolling meetings covering larger areas. This system has been deployed to limited degrees by some UK local authorities, particularly during Hazel Blears' tenure as Secretary of State for Communities and Local Government.[1] But despite a 2008 Government White Paper

looking to extend the practice, neither Labour nor Tory government has ever shown any real readiness to extend participatory
budgeting outside of very small ring-fenced budgets, which have
dwindled into non-existence under conditions of general austerity. It's therefore unsurprising that the public has shown little interest. This is a good example of a policy that can only have any
real democratic efficacy if both properly resourced and implemented with political commitment. There's also no reason why
it couldn't be facilitated considerably through the creative de-
ployment of online technologies. At its best a radical agenda informed by such ideas would take inspiration from the democratic
municipalism of movements and organisations like *Barcelona en
comú*, a 'citizens' platform' which is currently the governing party
of Barcelona, actively promoting an agenda of social equality and
participatory democracy.

The list of policies under this heading in the manifesto is
long and welcome: supporting social work training and looked
after children; reversing cuts and privatisation in the case of library services, children's protection services and post offices;
regenerating and supporting rural areas, defending local pubs;
regulating gambling and the impact of utility companies on the
local environment; protecting local government pensions. All of
it displays a justified confidence in the capacity of governments to
improve lives and protect communities from corporate exploitation. What is missing is any real acknowledgement – even implic-
itly – that social change depends on actually building up forms of
democratic power which are appropriate to the challenges of 21st

century capitalism, rather than simply 'devolving' powers which central government is assumed already to hold.

TRANSPORT

This tone of half-hearted list-making which characterises the 'local communities' section contrasts sharply with the confidence and clarity of vision on the following pages. A Labour government will modernise and renationalise the rail system while allowing local authorities to do the same to the bus network. "A publicly owned railway system can be the backbone of our plans for integrated transport." This is the stuff that socialist dreams are made of, and could make a significant break with the long epoch which began in the 1960s, during which the UK rail network has suffered persistent contraction, deterioration and privatisation. HS2 will be implemented; commitments to the National Cycling Network will be honoured.

The nationalisation and central co-ordination of railways was a key plank of social democratic reform and socialist infrastructure policy in the first half of the 20th century. Arguably this once again tells us from where the political vision set out in the manifesto draws much of its inspiration. It is at its boldest and most confident when essentially promising to restore some of the key institutions of the centralised social-democratic state which dominated the politics of advanced capitalist economies in the postwar period. Even today, after the extraordinary technological and social changes of recent decades, there is no logical or evidential basis for rail privatisation: a rail network, like a national grid, is a natural monopoly, the private ownership of which can only ever be justified by the most extreme ideological commitment to neo-liberalism and privatisation for its own sake. Promising to restore the rail network to the legal and political status that it enjoyed before the 1990s is therefore welcome and necessary.

What might be added to such proposals to give Labour transport policy more of a 21st century character? On cycling, the manifesto offers no more commitment than the current government has already made. Surely reducing the dominance of the car over urban and suburban environments is a crucial step towards enabling many British citizens to lead 'richer lives', and surely more could be offered in terms of developing urban infrastructure to facilitate this? Many such localities are in desperate need of the kind of traffic reduction and cycling-enhancement schemes (featuring road closures to cars, massive increases in cycle storage, parking and hire facilities, etc.) which have characterised the recent 'mini-Holland' projects in several London boroughs. Electric cars are also surely a key feature of any likely transport system in decades to come, and further development of facilities in order to make their nationwide use more practicable would greatly contribute to reducing our dependence on fossil fuels. Hopefully, future policy documents will at least mention this likelihood and propose a socialist way forward, with a nationwide network of public-owned charging points, using electricity generated by entirely renewable sources.

ENVIRONMENT

The manifesto section under this heading is deceptively short, and manages to incorporate an impressive range of policies – and criticisms of Tory policy – into a few dense few paragraphs. Promising to plant a million trees and to reverse the Conservative policy of tearing up environmental regulations, it makes clear, once again, that government spending and regulation have a central role to play in combating environmental degradation and the commercial forces responsible for it. Improving air quality and offering a sustainable future to our fishing, farming and food industries are clear priorities, and again mark the difference in approach from that Conservative, Coalition and New Labour governments, all committed to implementing market 'solutions' – carbon trading initiatives, for example – to such areas of policy. (Ed Miliband's championing of 'feed-in tariffs', enabling householders to sell excess solar or wind-generated electricity back to the national grid at agreed rates, was a notable and pioneering exception). It is also worth noting that a large part of the manifesto's treatment of ecological issues actually comes in the separate section on energy policy.

Once again, however, this is clearly an economists' manifesto: stabilising our agricultural economy comes across as a far higher priority than fundamentally re-orienting our culture and society away from unsustainable forms of consumerism. There are two deeply interrelated issues at stake here. One is the broad philosophical issue of what kind of society the Labour Party envisages creating, and whether this vision really departs significantly from a slightly modernised version of the Britain of the 1950s and 1960s. This again feels very much like a version of socialism which the 1945-51 Labour government would have recognised and endorsed, focused heavily on using central government to make industrial production more efficient and better-regulated.

The entire critique of industrial consumer society which became such a prevalent feature of radical culture in the 1960s and 70s was motivated, as much as anything, by the perception that this form of society – even in its most socialistic iterations (in Eastern Europe or Scandinavia) – had reached a material limit, which was being registered by the unsustainable degradation of the planetary environment. This was not an entirely new claim, but in fact echoed the thinking of earlier generations of radical thinkers such as William Morris, who had warned of the alienating effects of urbanisation and industrialisation, envisaging a society in which access to a world of natural beauty would not be the singular preserve of the rich. This latter objective became heavily politicised with the struggles for access to wild land in the 1920s and 30s, culminating in the famous mass trespass on Kinder Scout, a popular hiking area in Derbyshire, in 1932, led by militant left-wing activists.

Although the manifesto states clearly that "the balance needs resetting", there's little trace of this lineage in the way that it discusses environmental issues, nor little indication that the fundamental arguments of green economics have really been taken on board at all. Ultimately, what is promised by the whole manifesto is a Keynesian strategy to promote and regulate economic growth while ensuring that its benefits are widely shared. The argument that this itself is now a simply misconceived approach to economic management, and that what is required to avoid ecological catastrophe is a radical re-orientation of economic priorities away from the industrial capitalist obsession with growth, is very widely shared by radical economists with an interest in ecological issues. Even if we don't accept the argument, it is still an important one for progressives to engage with, especially now it is becoming obvious that we have already entered into an era of catastrophic climate change.

Ultimately, of course, what a truly radical vision for Britain in the 21st century would include would be some moves actually to democratise decision-making, planning and economic priorities.

One of the preconditions for the triumph of Thatcherism in the 1980s was a widespread sense that the British state had become both bloated and bureaucratic – increasingly remote from the public that it was supposed to serve. We must be wary of presenting a vision of a future Britain which merely restores the centralised state to that condition. Simply restoring the power of central government to dictate the direction and nature of economic growth would not achieve the ultimate political aim of democratic socialists: a society within which people are far more able than now to take part in the decisions determining their economic futures. The questions of how much priority to ascribe to economic growth and how much to environmental protection, or of how to reconcile the two, should ultimately be questions determined not simply by a Labour treasury team, but by citizens across the country on an ongoing basis.

ANIMAL WELFARE

The manifesto states that "Labour's vision is for the UK to lead the world with high animal welfare standards in the wild, in farming and for domestic animals." This is a highly laudable aim which all Labour members will be proud to support. The reader will be relieved to learn that I am not going to propose that animals be democratically empowered to protect themselves in line with true principles of socialist multi-species participatory democracy.

CULTURE FOR ALL

This section of the manifesto opens as follows: "Britain's creative industries are the envy of the world, a source of national pride, a driver of inward investment and tourism, and a symbol of the kind of country we are now and aspire to be in the future. As Britain leaves the EU, we will put our world-class creative sector at the heart of our negotiations and future industrial strategy."

The problems here are in the very first clause. 'Creative industries' is not a neutral concept. The very idea of the 'creative industries', as distinct from 'the arts' or 'culture' was an invention of 1990s neoliberal policy, with its insistence that every area of social life be re-modelled along capitalist lines. The manifesto not only has no critique to make of this approach: it simply reproduces it as normative common sense. This is a dead end for any kind of truly radical political agenda. Any such programme must seek to reclaim our culture from its complete control by capitalism, the commercial sector and their agents. In the case of education, the manifesto seems to understand this. In the case of other areas of cultural production, it's not clear that it does.

From this perspective, the substance of the manifesto's proposals is at best ambiguous. It proposes a massive government investment in creative infrastructure. But it proposes that the 'creative clusters' that it will seek to create and fund will be modelled on enterprise zones. So again, the assumption that creative work can simply be understood as a form of commercial enterprise is apparently taken for granted.

It is important to understand that 30 years ago, such an assumption would have been regarded as shocking. This is not to say that cultural policy, even Labour cultural policy, in the post-war period was unproblematic. 'The arts' were largely administered in a patrician manner, with only the 'high' arts (classical music and theatre, for example) receiving regular funding, the assumption being that the best way to improve the cultural 'health' of the nation was to make the culture of the haute-bourgeoisie available to as many people as possible (but especially to the professional classes and the petit-bourgeoisie).

The most radical challenges to these assumptions came in the 1970s and 80s, especially under the Greater London Council in the early 1980s. At the GLC, funding was re-directed into community arts and the idea was promoted of creating infrastructure for all forms of creative activity – rehearsal and recording facilities for young people engaged with popular musical forms, for example. To some extent this was justified in terms of some hoped-for economic benefits, but these were clearly understood as secondary to the political and social benefits to be gained from a real democratisation of cultural production. While the manifesto carries something of both legacies, offering to support arts training in school for all young people, and proposing that the national creative infrastructure be administered by the Arts Council, it retains the founding assumption that all of this cultural activity is best understood as simply a form of economic activity. It is surely this assumption – one which the vast majority of ordinary people instinctively understand to be problematic – which any radical politics today must challenge.

One of the fundamental problems with this assumption, which again the manifesto reproduces, is the complacency which it tends to promote around the question of whether cultural output is actually any good or not. A truly radical approach to cultural policy must, at least in part, take into account a fact which has become commonplace among critics and general cultural observers, but which is entirely off-limits from the point of view of conventional, neoliberal thinking. That fact is that since the end of the 1990s, we have been living through a weird period of cultural stasis, in which, despite a revolution in technologies production and distribution, there have been almost no significantly new developments in music, the visual arts, literature, or even fashion, according to some commentators. The 'creative industries' may have been very profitable – but they haven't produced much in the way of actual creativity.

Is this an issue which any government could even address? It could – and a plan to do so successfully might not look that different from the proposals contained in the manifesto. But such a programme will not address the fundamental problems at stake as long as they continue to be based on the fundamental assumption of neoliberal cultural policy: that 'creative industries' is an adequate concept with which to understand the vast network of activities which produce the cultural life of a people. A truly progressive government would not simply seek to bolster our 'creative industries' – it would question why they have produced so much boring and repetitive culture in recent years, and ask what it would take to liberate culture from the dictates of industry and finance.

CONCLUSION

Overall, this section of the manifesto marks a significant step forward in terms of freeing Labour policy thinking from the dead weight of neoliberalism. But too much of it betrays a narrow perspective, which can either only imagine a non-neoliberal future as some kind of return to the post-war past, or which simply cannot think about policy in terms not ultimately informed by neoliberal assumptions. Labour must seek to draw on a far wider range of disciplines and ways of thinking – including sociology, ecology, cultural studies, political philosophy, history, critical social policy, as well as the lived expertise of its vast membership – if it is to develop a truly visionary programme for the next general election.

10. EXTENDING DEMOCRACY

David Beetham

MANIFESTO SUMMARY

A Labour Government will establish a constitutional convention to look at extending democracy locally, regionally and nationally. Long-term, the Second Chamber should be democratically elected; immediately, the hereditary principle should be scrapped and its size reduced. The Freedom of Information Act will be extended to cover private companies that run public services. The voting age will be lowered to 16 and the Lobbying Act, which gags charities, will be replaced with a tougher register of lobbyists.

Labour will create a Minister for England and restore regional offices to improve contact between central and local government. Public opinion will determine whether to have directly elected mayors in future devolution deals.

Labour is opposed to Scottish independence and a further referendum on this. Scotland will benefit from Labour policies, with a new Scottish Investment Bank making £20 billion available for local projects. We will set up an inquiry into blacklisting and urge the Scottish Government to hold an inquiry into the role of the Scottish police during the 1984-5 miners' strike.

Long-term reform is needed to ensure public spending reflects the needs of different parts of the country. We will build on the new Development Bank of Wales, using over £10 bn from Labour's proposed National Investment Bank. Legislation will be introduced to strengthen Welsh devolution, including over local policing.

Labour remains fully committed to the principles and structures of the Good Friday Agreement in Northern Ireland, working with all sides to deliver real peace and prosperity.

***

It is a privilege to be taking part in these reflections on Labour's manifesto, which overturned the conventional wisdom that manifestos don't matter because, like the wider election campaign of which they form a part, they don't supposedly change the outcome. This one certainly did. I'm also delighted at the section on democracy, perhaps less for what it contains than that it is included in the first place. When the Blair Government published successive White Papers introducing its important constitutional reforms – on devolution, the Human Rights Act, Freedom of Information and many more – the D word was notable by its absence. They were all introduced under the rubric of 'modernisation'. This characterisation was unfortunate in that it forfeited the opportunity to link the reforms in a principled way, which could have provoked a wider reflection on what kind of democracy we had, or might aspire to. It also set limits to some of the reforms themselves. So, for example, 'modernising' the House of Lords clearly required eliminating the hereditary peers, or most of them, but still left in place their appointment by party leaders, which resulted in a grossly inflated number and the suspicion that peerages could be bought by sufficiently large party donations.

These constitutional reforms of the Blair era, extensive and necessary as they were, provoke another reflection. Successive opinion surveys revealed that, in parallel with the reforms taking effect, public confidence in representative democracy at Westminster was experiencing a continuous decline. Some of this decline can no doubt be attributed to key events, such as the decision on the Iraq war in the face of widespread public opposition, or the MPs' expenses revelations. But it also showed that constitutional reforms in themselves do not influence the public consciousness unless they can be shown to relate in some way to people's lived experience. And when Gordon Brown began his premiership in 2007 with a Green Paper announcing a further set of constitutional reforms, to "help renew trust and confidence in our democratic institutions", no attempt was made to explain why the much more extensive reforms of the Blair period had failed to do this.[1]

The manifesto proposal for a constitutional convention clearly marks the need to provide a popular basis for any further programme of institutional reform, such as was provided in

Scotland prior to devolution. It also acknowledges the difficulty of deciding what form of devolution might be acceptable and sustainable for England. Yet it is a pity that the idea of democracy in the manifesto has been limited to constitutional issues, and extending democracy to further institutional reform.

DEMOCRATIC PRINCIPLES

The concept of democracy embodies two distinct principles or ideals. One is that of popular influence or control over the collective decisions that affect people's lives, not only at the governmental level, but in the wider reaches of the economy and civil society – the network of associations and organisations that are a vital part of any representative system. The second principle is that of political equality, or equality of citizenship: everyone should "count for one and none for more than one", in the words of the 18th century philosopher Jeremy Bentham. No one should be disadvantaged because of their gender or ethnic or other identity, nor especially privileged in public affairs because of their wealth or social status.

Now it is perfectly possible for these two principles to come into conflict with each other. This can be seen, historically, in direct forms of democracy from ancient Athens to the Swiss cantons, where women's exclusion was deemed necessary because their domestic labour was needed to enable men to participate directly in political decision-making. And in more recent times popular majorities have sometimes sought to exclude particular minorities from equal citizenship. That is why we need a form of democracy in practice which gives equal weight to both principles. This was well put by the legal philosopher Ronald Dworkin when arguing in the 1990s for the incorporation of the European Convention on Human Rights into UK law. "True democracy," he wrote, is one in which "majority decision is legitimate only if it is a majority within a community of equals. That means not only that everyone must be allowed to participate in politics as an equal, through the vote and through freedom of speech and protest, but that political decisions must treat everyone with equal concern and respect, that each person must be guaranteed fundamental civil and political rights no combination of other citizens can take away, no matter how numerous they are or how much they despise his or her race or morals or way of life."[2]

This is why democracies need a framework of guaranteed rights upheld by an independent judiciary. And when judges uphold them, even against majority public opinion, they are defending democracy rather than undermining it, much less acting as 'enemies of the people'.

If we take these two principles together – popular control and equality of citizenship – then it is evident that the whole of Labour's 2017 manifesto was imbued with a strong democratising spirit. This spirit can be seen, for example, in the proposals for expansion of the cooperative sector, for workers' involvement in executive boards, for the recognition of trade unions and guarantees for workers' rights, all of which involve the extension of democracy to the workplace. It is also seen in the definition of Labour as the party of equality, of women's rights and the rights of minorities, and of all those subject to discrimination, including welfare recipients defined as 'skivers' and subjected to degrading and punitive assessments of eligibility. It can be seen further in proposals for enriching citizens' experience of the public realm, through extending access to culture, ensuring media plurality, promoting lifelong education, developing public libraries as knowledge hubs and protecting community centres and other public spaces.

It could have helped give greater coherence to these otherwise disparate elements of the manifesto if its democratising spirit had been made explicit, rather than being left implicit. Doing so could also have served to justify some of the constitutional proposals in the democracy section, such as extending Freedom of Information to private companies delivering public services, or removing restrictions preventing charities from campaigning in the run-up to an election. Both of these measures could be presented as enhancing the political influence of citizens, in the same way that electing the second chamber of Parliament and extending voting rights to sixteen year olds more obviously do. Gordon Brown's Green Paper of 2007 had particularly deplored the continuing decline in youth voting, yet his proposed constitutional reforms would not have reversed this, any more than exhortations to the young to "appreciate the importance of the democratic process and the need for active citizenship."[3] In retrospect, the greatest contribution of the manifesto to extending democracy was in offering young people and other reluctant voters a radical programme worth voting for, combined with the effective electoral mobilisation undertaken by countless volunteers. Together these contributed more to boosting voter turnout than any constitutional reforms could do.

This is not to discount institutional reform altogether; only that we need to be clear what difference it will make, if any, to citizens' lives and capacities. In this spirit the rest of this chapter will examine the salience of three possible constitutional reforms, one of which is given a central place in the democracy section of the manifesto, one which is only touched on, and one which is absent altogether.

DEVOLUTION WITHIN ENGLAND

Devolution to Scotland, Wales and Northern Ireland marks one of the successes of the Blair governments, and has given their peoples a more direct and secure ownership of the policies made in their name. The repatriation of EU powers from Brussels provides the opportunity for at least some of these to be vested in the devolved administrations, rather than centralised at Westminster. It also poses the crucial problem of how the terms of the Good Friday agreement can be maintained, when these have already been destabilised by the Tories' regressive alliance with the Democratic Unionist Party, like them a determined Brexit advocate in the face of majority opinion in the Province and fears of a hard border with the Republic.

A much more longstanding difficulty concerns what form of political devolution is feasible for England. That some form of devolution is needed is widely recognised. England remains an over-centralised polity, made worse by the continuous evisceration of local government. The situation becomes more unacceptable the more powers and resources are granted to the devolved administrations. England is too large as it stands to form a component of a possible federal constitution with the other nations. And there is a pressing need to rebalance the economies, life-chances and health prospects of the different parts of England, to which a viable system of political devolution could significantly contribute. The difficulty lies in reaching agreement on what such a system might be.

Two competing models divide opinion on the issue of English devolution. One is the city region, with or without an elected mayor on the London model. This concept was given constitutional status in 1974 with the Tory creation of the metropolitan counties in the major conurbations. They were subsequently disbanded under Margaret Thatcher, not because they were ineffective, but because they had not realised the partisan goal of ensuring a Tory presence in city administration. The concept was kept alive by informal relations between some of the district authorities on matters of common interest, such as planning and transport. It was revived under George Osborne, but in a haphazard manner, with separate negotiations with each potential combined authority. Some are already becoming a fact of life; but their revival does nothing to deal with the huge areas of the country, both urban and rural, which are not covered, and which contain some of the most deprived, and also some of the richest, parts of England.

The other model is the regional authority, covering the whole of an English region, and typically with a separately elected assembly and executive overseeing revived Regional Development Agencies. These would be comprehensive, including every part of the country, rural and urban. They would be comparable in population size to Wales, Scotland and Northern Ireland, and thus feasible components of a future federal system. This was the model advocated by John Prescott when he was Deputy Prime Minister, and trialled in a referendum in the North East, where it was decisively rejected by the electorate. Different explanations for this rejection have been given. The proposal offered derisory powers to the new authority, reportedly at the insistence of the Treasury. People were not enthusiastic about having another tier of elected councillors. And there was no sense of a common historic identity across such a large regional space.

Whether the manifesto proposal of a constitutional convention would be able to reconcile proponents of these divergent models, or overcome the defects inherent in each, must be open to question. To secure public support for any form of devolution would require guaranteeing that the new authorities had sufficient powers and resources to make a difference, and to do so in a way that was appropriate to the specific needs and wishes of their respective populations. Would the Treasury as presently constituted allow this?

DEMOCRACY, WEALTH AND CORPORATE POWER

Nothing does more to challenge the principle of political equality or distort the democratic process than the dominant influence exercised by the economically powerful over the policies of the Westminster government. This can be seen, for example, in the subordination of public health to corporate interests, in the history of successive privatisations, in the light touch afforded to tax avoidance and off-shore tax havens, in the toleration of the gig economy, in the subordination of foreign policy to arms manufacturers and so on. The answer lies not only in the reversal of specific policies, as the manifesto promises, but in a recognition of how far the corporate and financial sectors and their agents have become embedded at the heart of government.

Individual proposals in the manifesto, such as reform of the upper chamber of Parliament and a tightening of the rules on lobbying, address aspects of the problem; but they do so in a piecemeal fashion, whereas the problem is systemic, operating through multiple layers of governance and many different modes of influence. Direct modes of influence over policy, besides the financing of political parties and the advantage that wealth gives in lobbying, involve the insertion of business interests into the heart of government. This is not just through preferential access to ministers and top civil servants. It occurs through the increasing appointment of corporate personnel to high level civil service positions; through the development of departmental boards staffed by business executives; through the dominant presence of corporate representatives on government advisory bodies and task forces; through a complex of government-private sector partnerships. If this form of the revolving door between government and business could be described as 'revolving in', there is also 'revolving out', when higher civil servants, ministers and armed forces top brass take up lucrative positions on retirement in the businesses with which they had dealings when in public service. And the revolving door is particularly well-oiled when those who have revolved in revolve out again to take up top positions in their former industries.

These different modes of influence and control over public policy are fully documented in a 2011 Democratic Audit report *Unelected Oligarchy: Corporate and Financial Dominance in Britain's Democracy.*[4] For the financial sector in particular the book of the same year by Nicholas Shaxson, *Treasure Islands,* is worth reading, with its sobering conclusion: "Off-shore is at work nearby. It is undermining your elected government, hollowing out its tax base and corrupting its politicians."[5] Reading such works should not give rise to pessimism, much less inaction. But they do provide a salutary reminder of the obstacles that would confront a Labour government in implementing a radical economic and social agenda such as the manifesto contains.

Some of these obstacles could be mitigated by administrative measures, such as: radically altering the balance of interests and personnel involved in departmental consultations and advisory bodies; expanding the expertise of the civil service to lessen its dependence on business executives and private consultants; substantially extending the time that must elapse before government personnel can take up jobs in companies with which they had dealings in office. Some measures would require legislation, such as tightening the regulations on lobbying, or reforming party finance to drastically limit the size of allowable donations, and possibly adding public financing in proportion to registered party memberships. Such measures, taken together, would form a coherent programme for extending democracy, and would help to underpin the policies that would make a real difference to people's lives.

PROGRESSIVE ALLIANCE AND ELECTORAL REFORM

While it would be rash to make any predictions in the current political climate, the idea of another early general election allowing Labour 'one more heave' to electoral success looks highly improbable, for a number of reasons. First, the Tories will be in no hurry to trigger another election after the debacle of the last one, and there is no constitutional requirement for a new party leader to go to the country once installed as PM. Second, the new boundary changes and reduced number of MPs will substantially benefit the Tories after they come into operation in 2018. Third, it cannot be assumed that the organised tactical voting which worked to Labour's advantage in June 2017 will necessarily be repeated. Finally, Labour also benefited in June from a studied ambiguity over Brexit which cannot be sustained as the time for our exit from the EU draws nearer.

Let us suppose that political energies are not totally consumed over the coming period in avoiding a political split over Brexit, and that Labour is able to forge an agreed position which will hold the majority of the party together. This is already prefigured in Keir Starmer's policy announcement on 27th August that membership of the single market and customs union could continue under Labour in any transitional period, and possibly later if agreement on moderating freedom of movement could be achieved. Whatever the eventual position, the first three points above would make the idea of a progressive alliance with an electoral pact increasingly attractive, involving the Greens, left nationalist parties and the Liberal Democrats, once the latter have abandoned the regressive policies which proved so disastrous under their coalition with the Tories.

Part of such an alliance could be an agreement on electoral reform, along the lines of the system that has proved attractive and sustainable for the Parliament in Scotland and Assembly in Wales. The first-past-the-post system has serious defects, which have prevented it from ever being introduced for a new parliament or new or restored democracy anywhere in the world. It leads to quite arbitrary outcomes, depending on how the votes happen to be distributed between the different constituencies. It fails to reflect the pluralism of political opinion in the country, as smaller parties with significant electoral support are excluded from Parliament. It concentrates party attention on a small number of swing voters in marginal seats. Above all, it leads to voters in safe seats feeling that their votes don't count as they have no effect on the outcome. In the face of these defects, the one advantage proclaimed by its proponents – that it produces strong and stable single party rule – has been undermined by the results of the last three general elections in the UK.[6]

If such a reform were highlighted in the respective manifestos, there would be no need to put it to another referendum. It could be readily presented, not as serving narrow party interests, but as empowering citizens, since each vote would now count equally, wherever you lived. After all, one of the comments frequently made by voters in the North of England in the EU referendum was that for the first time in a UK poll their vote really counted because it could make a difference to the result. In this sense the reform could serve as a genuine extension of democracy.

11. A MORE EQUAL SOCIETY

Malia Bouattia

MANIFESTO SUMMARY

A Labour government will enhance the powers of the Equality and Human Rights Commission, strengthening its independence and accessibility to working class people. We will reinstate the public sector equality duties and seek to extend them to the private sector.

Ours will be a government for women, with at least 50% women in the Cabinet. We will gender audit all policy and legislation for its impact on women before implementation and defend abortion rights, seeking to extend them to Northern Ireland. We will appoint a Violence Against Women Commissioner, who will enforce minimum standards in tackling domestic and sexual violence and guarantee funding for refuges. In the face of rising maternity and pregnancy discrimination, we will scrap unfair employment tribunal fees and extend the time limit for applying for maternity discrimination to six months. Labour will work with the Health and Safety Executive to make mandatory a workplace risk assessment for pregnant women.

A Labour government will reform the Gender Recognition Act and the Equality Act 2010 to ensure they protect Trans people. We will bring the law on LGBT hate crimes into line with hate crimes based on race and faith and ensure all teachers receive training in tackling bullying of LGBT young people and ensuring relationships and sex education is LGBT inclusive. Likewise, we will ensure all frontline health and social care professionals receive training to meet the needs of LGBT people. Labour will ensure that NHS England completes the trial programme to provide PrEP quickly, and fully roll out the treatment to high-risk groups to help reduce HIV infection.

We will end racism and discrimination against Gypsy, Roma and Traveller communities. We will benefit black and Asian workers by introducing equal pay audit requirements on large employers and by making the minimum wage a living wage. We will implement the Parker Review recommendations to increase ethnic diversity on the boards of Britain's largest companies.

Labour will incorporate the UN Convention on the Rights of Persons with Disabilities into UK law. Tackling discrimination, we will legislate to make terminal illness a protected characteristic under the Equality Act and work to improve awareness of neurodiversity. Labour will make British Sign Language a recognised language.

***

We are living through difficult times, to say the least. Everywhere we turn in British society, from welfare to education, from security to civil liberties, there have been considerable reversals of past social gains. The Tory government has successfully cut and divested from lifelines for communities across the country. The National Health Service has been underfunded to the point of crisis, with the Red Cross having to come to many hospitals' rescue because the lack of resourcing left patients' lives at threat, bringing us closer and closer to a privatised system that would leave the poorest unable to access any healthcare.[1] In education, we have seen the progressive academisation of primary and secondary schools, severe cuts and job losses in further education colleges and the tripling of university tuition fees. Vital services, such as women's shelters, have been shut down[2] and the numbers of deported or detained migrants are ever-growing in Theresa May's obsessive race to control migration figures.[3] Benefits have been cut from the poorest[4], and disabled people have been put through degrading tests so that the state may decide whether they are 'disabled enough' for support.[5] In sum, there have been considerable blows to every institution that serves as a foundation for a more equal and just society. With the gap between rich and poor widening, oppression and discrimination inevitably increases as well.

Over the last decade, communities of colour have been faced with growing racism. Since the EU referendum, hate crime has risen considerably.[6] With some of the most racist policies being championed and made into law by our Government in the form of the Prevent agenda, some would say it's no surprise. Under the guise of the War on Terror, civil servants, doctors, teachers, social workers, counsellors and lecturers are all forced to undergo a training that encourages suspicion of 'the other' – read Muslim – and racial profiling.[7] The state has legitimised an Islamophobic rhetoric that paints all Muslims as an inherent threat because of their supposed innate desire for violence. This has given racists of all stripes a confidence boost, which in turn has led to burned mosques[8], the ripping of hijabs from Muslim women's heads, a van mowing down worshippers, and marchers in the streets chanting white supremacist slogans, often with police protection.[9] Government policies have meant the normalisation of Islamophobia to the extent that toddlers as young as four are being suspected of terrorism.[10] Muslims and people of colour have not been the only victims; Prevent has given the Government the ability to curtail everyone's civil liberties. Political movements have also been affected, as activists from anti-fracking campaigns, free education groups and even those working on humanitarian efforts for Palestinian children and refugees face interrogation.[11]

Alongside the bias and stereotyping motivated through often obligatory training, education spaces continue to suffer institutional racism. This is expressed in interactions in the classrooms, as well as the content of our studies, which is neither reflective of our diverse society nor honest about the role of the British Empire in the global south. All of this is of course demonstrated by the ongoing attainment gaps and retention problems across every level of the system, a crisis that has existed for over 60 years.[12]

LABOUR IN THE CAMP OF SOCIAL EXCLUSION

All this of course has not been only the result of the Conservative Government. For my generation, the Labour Party hasn't so much been associated with the golden years of the welfare state and the formation of the NHS, nor as a party with organic links to a powerful and well-organised trade union movement. It hasn't really even figured in our political life as a mass organisation that has delivered at times important reforms for the vast majority of working people, despite remaining limited on questions of anti-racism or anti-sexism. By the time I became political, in the early 1980s, the Greater London Council and the shift away from radical action from below in favour of institutionalised liberation politics, seemed like a different era.

The Labour Party for my generation is associated with destructive attacks on welfare services, black communities, and the poor. My entry into politics and my first political memories, thoughts, and actions formed around the early stages of privatisation in the health service and the introduction of university fees after being promised 'Education, Education, Education' – both carried out under a Labour Government.[13]

More than anything else, my generation's formative political experiences were the invasions of Afghanistan and Iraq, and the announcement of the so-called War on Terror. Millions marched, schoolchildren walked out and trade unions mobilised workers for the first time in decades. We were faced with violent aggression abroad and increased surveillance and criminalisation at home. It was the Labour Party that justified the bloodshed in the Middle East, while launching the Prevent agenda in the UK.[14]

What all these policies had in common is that they targeted and hit the poorest and most vulnerable in society the hardest. The rolling back of the welfare state and the increased privatisation of care is disproportionately hitting women – effectively expected to step in where the state retreats. Increased surveillance and criminalisation is concentrated on communities of colour. Similarly, the growing marketisation of post-16 education – characterised by rising fees and falling financial support – has hit working class and black communities the hardest.

The Thatcher-Reagan era was followed by the Clinton-Blair years. The process of defeat for labour and liberation movements was followed by the institutionalisation of a new regime of societal organisation, in which racialised communities, the poor, and women bore the brunt of the new social reality, and where social democratic organisations – the Labour Party leading the way – used their historic link to the working class and social movements to impose growing repression and inequality. Loic Wacquant (2009) has described these dual processes, amongst others, as the two phases of neoliberalism: first, the rollback phase with its destruction of the gains of previous generations and the defeat of organised grassroots movements, followed by the roll-out phase and the organisation of a new societal model, where solidarity and collective care were decisively replaced by individual responsibility.[15] The most striking illustration of this process in the British context is the fact that both Thatcher and

Blair, when asked what their greatest achievement was, both answered: New Labour.[16]

The party that fought in Parliament to make the welfare state and the NHS a reality became, in the space of half a century, the party that could deliver its dismantling. This had consequences on the ground and in social movements too. When I was a student, it was unthinkable for activists, or simply for people who cared about social justice, to join Labour. In the student movement Labour students were associated (and often still are) with the most conservative political stances. This was illustrated well by Wes Streeting's presidency of the National Union of Students.

While students were being radicalised through their opposition to the war, growing solidarity with the people of Palestine, the occupation of over thirty campuses in 2009 against the assault on Gaza and the growing resistance to campus job losses and department closures, the NUS under Streeting – that is under the Labour Party – fought against these developments with all its might. Streeting denounced the student occupations and even met with Israeli officials responsible for the Gaza attack. He condemned lecturers taking strike action and declared that students needed industrial action "like a hole in the head."[17]

It was no surprise then for many who became politically conscious and active in the new millennium that Labour, under the leadership of the supposedly 'Red Ed' Miliband, stood for election on a platform that not only ignored the concerns of oppressed communities in the UK, but actively proposed to increase the attacks against them. Both Prevent and greater restrictions on immigration featured as central elements in his manifesto.[18] The message was made even clearer through the now infamous 'migration' mug: Labour remained firmly in the camp of social exclusion.[19] In case anybody was still in doubt, its xenophobia was even carved into a huge slab of concrete. It was – literally – set in stone.[20]

ADDRESSING INEQUALITY

For many therefore, it was a positive surprise to see a Labour party entering the General Election in 2017 with a manifesto that dedicated an entire section to A More Equal Society. The opening alone outlines some of the urgent issues that plague our society and hinder us from reaching a state of liberation free of structural oppression. It is refreshing that the section steers away from tokenism by carefully reflecting on four areas: Women, LGBT Equality, Diverse Communities, and People with Disabilities.

Women's liberation is not described as a mission limited to the UK, but a global one. From ending violence against women which leaves one in three dead worldwide – and two a week in the UK – to addressing maternity discrimination more actively, the manifesto emphasises the importance of destroying all traces of misogyny, as it is literally a matter of life and death.[21]

Similarly, LGBT Equality with its mention of Trans liberation, and taking on ableism through the lens of the social model of disability, all show an on-the-ground understanding of the barriers faced by self-defining people. We have long witnessed failed promises to take on oppression through deficit model-based solutions, which focus on individual inadequacies and minimise the structural issues involved, instead of active engagement with affected communities and movements. LGBT activists demonstrate against state repression, yet increased police at Pride marches would be seen as the solution to threats of homophobia.[22] This crucial section of the manifesto finally echoes the radical alternatives that people have long fought for on the streets.

It is, however, disappointing that following the first lines of A More Equal Society, that "The Labour Party is the party of equality and seeks to build a society and world free from all forms of racism, anti-Semitism and Islamophobia," the extended portion on this is entitled Diverse Communities. Whilst it is important to celebrate the diversity of our society, the rise of the far right across Europe and white supremacist violence as well as the election of fascists in governments worldwide call for the use of a language that relates to this reality.

Furthermore, whilst the strategy for tackling anti-Semitism is exemplary, there is little substance on plans to dismantle other forms of racism. Black and Asian communities are only mentioned in relation to discrimination in the workplace and as valuable contributors to the UK economy through small business ownership. I am not suggesting that these aren't issues faced by these communities, but the promise to end racism should not be on the basis of the labour we provide.

Given the years of Black Lives Matter protests against police brutality sweeping the country[23], some of the largest refugee solidarity marches organised against the drowning of migrants in the Mediterranean sea[24], the bringing of central London to a standstill when thousands stood against Trump's Muslim ban[25] and the opposition of all teaching unions to Prevent[26], one might have expected these experiences to be reflected in the policies proposed.

The promises for addressing inequality are undoubtedly welcome and indicate the powerful impact of liberation movements globally. The numerous references to class and poverty as contributors to systematic discrimination felt by diverse groups also indicate an intersectional approach to both the problems and solutions.

A CENTRAL CONTRADICTION

This tension between a new beginning and limited policy goals represents an important contradiction in the new realities in Labour. Indeed, if the Labour Party's historic links to the labour and social movements allowed it to play a central role in the imposition of a new societal order, the same links had a contradictory effect in the long term. The irony of the rise of Corbynism is that the very social base that is making his leadership – and possible Prime Ministerial role – a reality are the social forces that developed in opposition to the politics that were born under Blair.

It is the activists from the social movements of the last decades – the anti-war movement, the Palestine solidarity

movement, the student revolt against fees and the re-mobilisa-
tion of a section of the trade union movement in the face of austerity – as well as those inspired by them but frustrated by their
defeat – that have turned to the Labour Party. Labour branches
are being flooded with the organisers of the very movements that
fought to halt or reverse the policies of the Blair era. This irony is
perfectly captured in the attempts by the unelected Labour machine to suspend new members who have criticised the party and
its leadership in the past, when it is this very fact that has given
the current leadership of the party its credibility.[27]

Here also lies the contradiction of Corbynism. If the social
base for his sudden inspiring rise is the social movements of the
recent past, it is also important that they have (re)turned to the
Labour Party largely following their defeat, rather than on the
heels of success. The danger then is that all hopes are pinned on
Corbyn and his electoral victory, without a longer-term vision of
the kind of social pressure from below that will be necessary to
make his programme a reality.

His programme further captures this contradiction. It is
both a qualitative and quantitative giant step forward in terms
of questions of liberation in comparison with what was on offer under Miliband. At the same time, it also shows the need for
the Corbyn leadership to act as a counterbalance to the right of
the Labour Party, and its lack of confidence in being able to roll
back fully the consequences of years of reactionary policies and
so-called common sense. This tension between left-wing electoral successes and an organisational weakness on the ground, in

unions and movements up and down the UK, lies at the heart of the challenges we will face in the months and years to come. I have had a personal taste of it on a much smaller scale. My election as president of NUS represented a sharp break with the old status quo described above. It represented a similar electoral culmination of years of new movements in the student world, which wanted a political leadership that stood for free education, international solidarity and an active strategy of links with the trade union movement. Unfortunately, this electoral victory could not be turned into mobilisations on the ground that would have been able to wash away the remnants of the past in the union machine, as well as turn the tide in colleges and campuses across Britain.

Corbyn, through the development of Momentum and the mass rallies he has been able to generate up and down the country, has been able to lay the foundations to defeat the old forces in the machine. His ability to turn the excitement into mobilisation and action, however, remains to be seen. His manifesto reflects this reality very clearly. It is an unrecognisable Labour Party to the one I grew up under. It is one that inspires hope and breathes confidence. It is also one which still hovers between the future and the past. It is our collective movements in workplaces, communities and the streets that will decide whether it steps decisively into a new period, or remains stuck in the past.

Malia Bouattia wishes to thank Sai Englert for his help with this chapter.

12. A GLOBAL BRITAIN

Glen Rangwala

MANIFESTO SUMMARY

A Labour Government will put conflict resolution and human rights at the heart of foreign policy.

In Israel/Palestine, Labour is committed to a negotiated two-state solution peace deal. We will push to secure a resolution of the conflicts in other regions, while using all lawful means possible to confront the threat of Daesh. We will review all training and equipment contracts with repressive regimes, to ensure that Britain never colludes in the mistreatment of civilians. We will stand up for the rights of citizens in Britain's overseas territories, in particular supporting the right of the Chagos islanders to return to their homelands. We will reclaim Britain's leading role in tackling climate change and strengthen our commitment to the UN, while seeking to reform it to make it more responsive. We will appoint dedicated global ambassadors on women's and LGBT rights and religious freedom.

While supporting the contribution our defence industry makes to the UK economy, we also believe that strong export controls are vital and will therefore cease arms exports to countries where they may be used to violate international humanitarian law. Specifically, we will demand an independent, UN-led investigation into alleged violations in Yemen, as well as an independent inquiry into Britain's military role in the 1984 raid on the Golden Temple in Amritsar.

Labour will order a complete strategic defence and security review, while maintaining our commitment to NATO and to spending at least 2% of GDP on defence. Labour supports the renewal of the Trident nuclear deterrent. We will publish a Defence Industrial Strategy White Paper, including a National Shipbuilding Strategy to secure a long-term future for the industry, workers and UK defence. A Labour Government will examine recruitment and retention policies for the Armed Forces, driving up standards in Service Accommodation.

In International Development, Labour will ensure aid is used to reduce poverty, not make corporate profits. We will implement a cross-government strategy to ensure the Sustainable Development Goals are achieved and our obligations on the refugee crisis are met. We will reinstate the Civil Society Challenge Fund to support civil society organisations, work to tighten the rules governing corporate responsibility and establish a Centre for Universal Health Coverage. Labour will act decisively on tax havens, introducing strict standards of transparency for crown dependencies and overseas territories.

***

MANIFESTOS AND FOREIGN POLICY

Party manifestos tend not to say very much about foreign and defence policy. The conventional wisdom is that there are few votes to be won through pronouncements about foreign affairs, save for those about relations with the European Union, an issue which straddles domestic and foreign agendas and which has its fierce partisans. Instead, for relations outside of Europe, the section in a manifesto on foreign and defence affairs has become little more than an opportunity to signal general competence, to affirm patriotic credentials, and to have a dig at one's opponents.

The Conservative manifesto of 2017 is not untypical in this regard. It makes few specific policy proposals. Its sections on foreign and defence policy mention only one other country – the United States – and one region – Europe. Instead, that manifesto makes a fairly overt appeal to nationalist sentiments, by repeatedly making reference to Britain's global pre-eminence, and by positioning itself in an international leadership role. Indeed, the phrase 'lead the world' or variants of that phrase appears in six consecutive sentences at one point, with no information on how that leadership would be established or for what purpose. It indicates not just poor drafting skills of the manifesto-writers, but a lack of serious thinking about what foreign policy is for, other than self-aggrandisement.

The point is not just to criticise the way in which inflated claims came to be a poor substitute for substantive policies from the governing party before the 2017 elections. A review of recent manifestos from any of the three major parties over recent decades would find a similar lack of depth in the discussion of foreign policy. Perhaps the only exception was the 2010 Labour manifesto, but in that, the detail was all about the past – what Gordon Brown's government had already achieved, rather than about what it would do in the future.

The 2017 Labour manifesto shares most of a title with the foreign policy section of the Conservative manifesto – 'Global Britain' – but that is almost the only point of convergence. What is striking instead about the 2017 Labour manifesto is its close reference to major issues in world politics, and the specific ideas it presents for engaging with them. A manifesto which on the first page of its foreign policy section mentions the food crisis in the Sahel – probably the single most pressing humanitarian issue in the world today, but which is desperately underreported – demands to be taken seriously.

The manifesto itself divides its account into three sections: diplomacy, defence and development. Perhaps a more instructive way to understand it is to divide the manifesto between the single-issue policies, oriented around specific claims to economic or social justice, and the more general approach to foreign policy contained with the Labour Party programme. The first of those identifies and prioritises themes that have been neglected or forgotten by political parties, but which have been kept alive by advocacy campaigns inside and outside the Labour Party. The second, setting out a way in which foreign policy would be conducted, is still more ambitious and potentially innovative.

WHAT'S THERE - PUTTING WRONGS TO RIGHT

Much of the current leadership of the Labour Party has a strong and historic affiliation to organisations campaigning for economic and social justice, both for those within the UK marginalised by the globalisation and financialisation of the world economy, and those around the world whose lives and communities have been imperilled by violence and environmental destruction. It was no surprise therefore to see prominent references to these issues in the foreign policy section of the manifesto. It pledges, among other things, to support the return of the Chagos islanders to their homelands, an inquiry into alleged British involvement under the Thatcher government in the Golden Temple massacre in Amritsar, a suspension of the arms trade with Saudi Arabia, and recognition of the state of Palestine.

Although these commitments will have resonance individually only to a relatively small proportion of the electorate – the issue of Israel/Palestine perhaps to more – their inclusion demonstrates the continued relevance of those groups who have been significant to the transformation of the Labour Party over recent years. None of the single-issue commitments in the 2017 manifesto appeared, for example, in the previous one, for Ed Miliband's 2015 campaign. Each of them speaks to a small but concerted group of activists, many of whom have disengaged from party politics over previous years, if not decades. Some of the commitments in the defence section of the manifesto can similarly be seen as coming out of campaigning affiliations: the National

Shipbuilding Strategy is one of many proposals throughout the manifesto that speaks to specific geographically concentrated communities that have suffered in the context of Britain's industrial decline.

When foreign policy proposals are made that are based on single issues, there are two standard criticisms that usually follow. First, sceptics argue that the resultant policies are driven by the need to be seen to be doing something, and so become exercises in posturing rather than actually achieving a more just or worthwhile outcome. And secondly, critics argue that taking issues in isolation means that policies do not fit into a broader, coherent and longer term framework of foreign policy. Both charges are relevant to parts of the Labour manifesto's foreign policy section, but there is also clearly more to it than simply assertions of advocacy.

An example is the three policies in the manifesto about the ongoing war in southern Arabia, which has been waged largely from the air and through blockade since March 2015, and led by the Middle East's richest country, Saudi Arabia, against its poorest, Yemen. Much of the critical attention from campaigning organisations and publications has gone on pressing for a cessation of UK arms sales to Saudi Arabia. While doing so would perhaps have some symbolic importance, the practical effect would be minimal: after all Saudi Arabia has recently signed the largest weapons deal in history, a ten-year programme with the Trump administration in the United States, and does not need UK weapons for its wars. When previously the Obama administration had suspended weapons sales, that show of disapproval seems to have had no effect on the Saudi government in their actual conduct of the war on Yemen either.

The manifesto does propose a suspension of the sale of weapons for use in the conflict. But it doesn't stop at that, and sets out two specific policies that would be more likely to be consequential if implemented. The first is to support a negotiation-based resolution to the Yemen conflict. Although this looks like a platitude, it comes out of the minimal international backing for peace talks that were held in late 2016, even when the prospects for compromise were there. The eventual failure of those talks was in large part due to the lack of external support for the proposed power-sharing scheme: international incentives if offered could have led to a deal. The second policy is to push to a comprehensive United Nations-led inquiry into violations of international humanitarian law in Yemen. That would push directly against Saudi Arabia's claims that it has always acted in accordance with its international obligations: what it brands the 'war of legitimacy' would be directly challenged by a finding that it has systematically violated the basic laws of war. That was why, when in 2016 a report to the United Nations Security Council listed Saudi Arabia as a country which violated children's rights, by launching attacks on schools in Yemen, the Saudi government threatened to withhold its funding to UN aid programmes – until the then UN Secretary-General, shamefully, relented and removed Saudi Arabia from the list of offenders.

The manifesto's content indicates that Labour's foreign policies go beyond a headline-grabbing stance when it comes to dealing with pressing issues in global politics. There is of course room for their further development. With the case of Yemen, the most widespread harm has come from not the air strikes but the comprehensive Saudi blockade on the country's ports which prevents basic goods from entering the country. While there are many international mechanisms and laws of war that attempt to regulate the damage caused to civilians through direct violence, there is comparably very little that deals with the suffering caused by blockades. A Labour policy that addressed how international mechanisms could be developed for monitoring blockades and limiting their humanitarian effects would be a significant advancement in setting out how diplomacy can be used to improve international security.

WHAT'S THERE – A DIFFERENT APPROACH TO FOREIGN POLICY

It is a hallmark of the manifesto that it proposes initiatives in diplomacy, defence and development to help establish international strategies for achieving collective benefits. It is this emphasis on multilateralism, and the importance of maintaining a means of promoting collective action within an increasingly polarised world, that provides the overarching framework for thinking about what a distinctively Labour foreign policy would be.

The British departure from the European Union cannot but create a suspicion from many around the world that the UK is becoming an isolationist, inward-looking country with little interest in international cooperation or global problems. The manifesto directly challenges that growing impression by setting out a different approach to foreign policy that is centred on the need for global cooperation, and presenting what Britain's role in this can be. This then is a diametrically opposed notion to what 'Global Britain' means in the Conservative manifesto. There it is used to indicate an implausible bid for 'leadership' on the international stage, redolent with themes of faded glory from an imperial past. In contrast, in the Labour manifesto it means that British and global interests are closely intertwined, and that successful strategies for improving security or well-being in Britain must draw in as wide a range of partners from around the world as possible. On issues as diverse as climate change, the refugee crisis, cyber security and tax evasion, the emphasis is on what Britain's specific role can be within wider global efforts. It recognises that major powers within the world are pulling in different, sometimes mutually hostile, directions. But this does not diminish the relevance of collective efforts to address common issues of concern: indeed, it makes them all the more important.

A good example in the manifesto is in highlighting the significance of tax havens in stymying both the finances of the British government and the prospects for international development, while also recognising that global action is needed. It rightly notes that capital flight from Africa to tax havens, many of which are British overseas territories and Crown dependencies, cost the continent ten times what it receives in aid. The government is ideally placed to take decisive action in ensuring transparency in UK offshore territories, and by doing so would both significantly boost the economies of developing countries and reduce inequality within the UK.

But dealing with tax havens requires concerted international efforts between many different countries – including in particular the Netherlands, Switzerland and Singapore, as well as the UK – which act as conduits for the transfer of capital without taxation to offshore jurisdictions. The manifesto's focus on how Britain can do much more to support multilateral attempts to solve global problems should take Labour policy on to thinking about how an effective sanctioning system can be developed for dealing with corporations and havens, one that goes beyond simply naming and shaming perpetrators.

The manifesto does not fall into the trap of taking a naïve view of international organisations by portraying them as the solution to the world's ills. It does make commitments to supporting the United Nations, including by aligning with the calls for the creation of a UN emergency peace service, and NATO. It retains though a much needed scepticism towards them, especially as they are organisations run principally by powerful countries for their own purposes.

There is instead a mix of different methods for achieving multilateral cooperation for shared interests. Some of these are partnership arrangements with progressive movements around the world, such as with trade unions and women's associations through a civil society fund. Others would be creating link points in the British government which would take a role in coordinating global efforts, such as a global ambassador for LGBTQ rights and a minister for peace and disarmament who would steer efforts for conflict prevention and post-conflict justice. It is this recognition that there are many different channels for advancing global cooperation in which the British government can play a role that marks the manifesto out as having a distinctive and consistent approach to foreign policy.

WHAT'S MISSING

The 2017 Labour manifesto has a different approach and a new set of issues that it raises. That also means that there are themes and commitments that have previously been in Labour manifestos which are no longer there.

The most apparent of these omissions are the wars in Iraq and Afghanistan. In the last three manifestos, there was a significant amount of text devoted to these, either trying to excuse those disastrous wars or to portray lessons learnt from them. Since the British withdrawal from Iraq in 2011 and the end of combat operations in Afghanistan in 2014, the wars which continue in both countries have receded from British public attention. Nevertheless, there is still a substantial UK military training operation in Afghanistan, and participation in air strikes against the self-styled Islamic State (IS) organisation in Iraq and Syria. The legacy in both countries of Britain's military involvement remains huge.

The 2017 manifesto makes a passing mention of learning from the Chilcot Inquiry, which was into the British role in the Iraq war, and later makes another brief reference to IS in Afghanistan and Iraq. This is not very much attention, but is still more than the Liberal Democrats or the Conservatives, neither of whom mention either Iraq or Afghanistan at all in their 2017 manifestos. A significant and direct British role in either country now would be counterproductive however well-meaning its intentions. But the absence of serious consideration of the legacy of two of the longest wars in British history or the devastating effect of those wars on the people living there is perhaps in tension with the Labour manifesto's confident articulation of the values of peace, international law and post-conflict justice.

If the absence of any significant reference to the wars in Iraq and Afghanistan can be seen as a way to avoid inflaming disagreements between Labour candidates during the election campaign, the short references to supporting the renewal of the Trident nuclear weapons system and the commitment to NATO are even more so. The manifesto does not commit a Labour government to a continuous at-sea nuclear capability, as the 2015 manifesto had done. Nor does it falsely label Trident as giving the UK 'independent' nuclear capability, as the previous three manifestos claimed. After all, the missiles are leased from a shared pool belonging to the United States, which manufactures, manages and maintains them.

Unless the fiction of an autonomous ability to use the missiles is believed, the rationale in spending at least £31 billion simply on renewing a nuclear weapons system is lost. With the explicit opposition of the Party leadership to the use of nuclear weapons under any circumstances, the inclusion of nuclear deterrence within the manifesto results in a lack of coherence in Labour's defence policy, one that its opponents will continue to exploit. The commitment to NATO, and the resultant acceptance of the pre-eminence of the United States in the organisation of defence within member countries, also stands in tension with a manifesto which labels the current US administration 'erratic' – the earlier draft of the manifesto text used the stronger term 'combative' – and which openly signals its willingness to disagree with US policies on the international stage.

A GLOBAL BRITAIN

Across the 2017 manifesto, there is a recognition that the British departure from the European Union will have wide-ranging consequences for communities across the country. Other sections of the manifesto present how a Labour government would mitigate some of the most negative consequences of that departure. The final section of the manifesto however is focused at its best on the opportunities for a different sort of foreign policy – one that has been spurred by the vote to leave the European Union, but is not defined by it.

The manifesto's approach to foreign policy is one that is centred on globally shared concerns. The well-being of British citizens is intimately tied to the grave challenges to security, the economy, the environment and human health across the world. It is these close linkages that the manifesto presents as the core field with which British foreign and defence policy should be most keenly engaged. The recognition of the relevance of these themes is what the manifesto means when it affirms the importance of 'keeping Britain global'.

The shared concerns are partly to be found in the justice-based issues that are manifest as violations of human rights or unresolved past wrongs. The manifesto has clearly defined proposals for many of these issues, particularly those with which Britain has economic, security or historic links. The central force of the manifesto's projected foreign policy however comes from the overarching project to make Britain a hub for multilateral efforts to tackle global problems in an increasingly polarised world. It is a project that stands in opposition to the isolationist stance of many powerful countries around the world, and in contrast to the unilateral and interventionist approach of others. The gap between the scale of common global problems and the limited means that exist to deal with those problems remains wide. In seeking to work concertedly at bridging that gap, Labour's foreign policy is well-focused, distinctive and ambitious.

AFTERWORD

Jon Lansman

A few weeks into the general election campaign, you could see things had started changing. Jeremy Corbyn addressed a crowd of 20,000 cheering concertgoers at the Tranmere Rovers stadium. The video went viral. Canvassers reported entire streets – in Conservative-held seats – bedecked with Labour banners, bartenders refusing to let campaigners pay for their own drinks, and hundreds of people spontaneously arriving for door-knocking sessions in all weathers. With a huge poll gap still to close, we studiously avoided runaway optimism. But the ground was already shifting.

It shifted due to a programme of hope in the manifesto that set out a clear vision and was counterposed to a dismal campaign promising another five years of cuts, falling wages and calculated misery. The programme took centre stage in a sensational turnaround that denied the Conservatives a majority.

The programme was carried into communities by Momentum, the grassroots pro-Corbyn Labour campaign organisation which matched an inspiring manifesto with an inspiring ground campaign, driven by tens of thousands of volunteers who believed passionately in what they were doing.

Elections are not won by air wars alone, and Nielsen's studies of US elections suggest a well-organised field operation can make a margin of difference of around 3-6%. These figures assume around a fifth of voters in a seat can be reached – in our case, Momentum canvassers were knocking on every single door from Sheffield to Battersea, Brighton to Crewe, Lancaster to Derby.

At the same time parts of the party machinery were piling resources into safe seats with majorities of 10,000. By the end of the campaign, many of Jeremy Corbyn's greatest sceptics in the parliamentary party recognised the contribution Momentum's organisers and activists had made to their return to Westminster.

When the snap general election was called, all of us were forced to think quickly of ways to deliver several months' worth of exhaustive work in a few weeks. Technological innovation, often on a shoestring, drove results. The My Nearest Marginal app we developed was used by over 100,000 people – almost four times Momentum's membership – to match themselves with the most useful canvassing sessions. Momentum contacted over 400,000 people on polling day through viral WhatsApp messaging. Throughout the election Momentum was able to act as a testbed for new campaigning techniques, and absorb practice from across the world, including a contingent from the Bernie Sanders campaign in the US. Phone canvassing technology used by both

Labour and the Conservatives was pioneered during Corbyn's leadership campaigns.

It is often taken as read that the left sweeps to victory in social media battlegrounds, but in the 2015 election commentators acknowledged widely that the Conservatives had an edge in targeted Facebook adverts. This time, nearly one in four UK Facebook users had viewed a Momentum video, with significant inroads made in key seats and among demographics unlikely to usually engage with Labour content.

This was achieved with less than £2,000 of advertising spending, compared to £1million by the Conservatives in 2015, and was reliant on exciting content with high production values, a viral strategy and an ecology of pro-Labour social media pages that helped boost output. The best-performing video was "Daddy, why do you hate me?" which looks back on more years of Theresa May from the perspective of a small child whose father voted Conservative.

Momentum, though, is much more than a viral content producer. The object of effective digital campaigning is to boost the reach and capacity of a movement. Before that, a movement has to be built – and that has meant ensuring that people enthusiastic about Corbyn have accessible routes to activism, engagement and the ability to help shape the movement.

People everywhere wanted to do their bit. But without Momentum, the structures for them to use their energy and skills productively would not have existed in the same way. The campaign we built was able to cover extensive ground – over fifty campaign days in key seats throughout the election, culminating in 10,000 pledges to take the day off on 8 June, and a total of 1.2 million doors knocked on. Critically, we worked hard to ensure that the engagement on doorsteps was meaningful.

Canvassing is too often a tick-box exercise, little more than data collection and a perfunctory attempt at persuasion. We held over forty training sessions across the country which equipped thousands of activists to communicate successfully, build empathy and find the issues that matter to the voter in question. Meanwhile organisers worked to ensure that new canvassers could get to know each other and build lasting connections.

The Labour manifesto provided trainers with their talking points, a rare example of a genuine mass-circulation political document. As one successful parliamentary candidate in a knife-edge marginal put it, "People were more informed about the manifesto than ever, and plenty of the broad themes came through. Fees, housing, utilities and rail, investment in the economy to create jobs… and the NHS and National Care Service also."

Momentum organisers began the election with thirty target seats on their hit list. Twenty-five are now in Labour hands. We delivered an unprecedented mass-movement campaign over less than fifty days, and since the general election, we haven't stopped. Our "hackathons" have brought together digital and design experts to stay at the cutting edge of political technology. Our "Unseat" campaign is putting hundreds on the ground in key Conservative-held marginals. And at the time of writing, we are preparing for the return of The World Transformed, a festival of ideas and discussion over several days running alongside Labour Party conference.

The organisation has few full-time staff, and survives mostly on the contributions of its members plus a few affiliated unions. And yet it has a strength not seen in British politics for a long time – huge numbers of everyday people, from all backgrounds, in all corners of the country, crying out for change and motivated by the promise of a society that works for the many, not the few.

Momentum was founded following Jeremy Corbyn's first leadership bid to capture the energetic, do-it-yourself spirit that fuelled the election and keep Labour's hundreds of thousands of new members engaged.

It aimed to bridge social movements and local initiatives with Labour's structures, revive grassroots-oriented culture in the party, and experiment with new and diverse approaches to engaging people and winning elections. On all those counts Momentum has proved its value, bringing fresh air and fresh thinking to the labour movement.

ABOUT THE CONTRIBUTORS

David Beetham was Labour councillor for Manchester Moss Side and a parliamentary candidate in the 1970s; succeeded Ralph Miliband as professor of politics at the University of Leeds in 1980; was a founding member of Democratic Audit in 1990. Books on democracy include *Democracy under Blair* (jointly, Abe Books, 2002) *Parliament and Democracy in the 21st Century* (Google, 2006) and *Democracy: a Beginner's Guide* (Abe Books, 2005).

Malia Bouattia is the former President of the National Union of Students, as well as having served as Black Students Officer for two years. She is the co-founder of the Black Women's Forum UK and the Students not Suspects/Educators not Informants Coalition against the Prevent agenda.

Gregor Gall is Professor of Industrial Relations at the University of Bradford, Editor of *Scottish Left Review* and Director of the Jimmy Reid Foundation. He has written or edited over twenty books, the most recent of which are *Bob Crow – fighter, leader, socialist: a political biography* (Manchester University Press, 2017) and *Employment Relations in Financial Services: an exploration of the employee experience after the financial crash* (Palgrave, 2017).

Jeremy Gilbert is Professor of Cultural and Political Theory at the University of East London, and editor of the journal *New Formations.* He was a member of the founding national committee of *Momentum* and is a member of the *Compass* management committee. He writes regularly for *The Guardian, Open Democracy, Red Pepper* and various other left publications. His most recent book is *Common Ground: Democracy and Collectivity in an Age of Individualism* (Pluto, 2014).

Dr Stuart Hodkinson is Associate Professor in Critical Urban Geography at the University of Leeds. His research focuses on neoliberal urban governance, austerity and contestation in relation to public housing, welfare reform, gentrification and the right to the city. Recent publications include Beswick J; Alexandri G; Byrne M; Vives-Miró S; Fields D; Hodkinson S; Janoschka M (2016) Speculating on London's housing future: The rise of global corporate landlords in 'post-crisis' urban landscapes, *City*, 20, pp.321-341 and Hodkinson S; Essen C (2015) Grounding accumulation by dispossession in everyday life: The unjust geographies of urban regeneration under the private finance initiative, *International Journal of Law in the Built Environment*, 7, pp.72-91.

Ewa Jasiewicz is a union and community organiser and author. She has worked with precarious and casualised workers in the

UK since 2005 for Unite the Union and now works as an organiser for the National Union of Teachers. She has been active in climate, social and economic justice movements and has undertaken solidarity work with people in Palestine, Syria, Afghanistan and Iraq. Her book *Razing* Gaza (*Podpalic Gaze*) was nominated for the Beata Pawlak Award in 2011.

Ruth Lister is a Labour peer and Emeritus Professor of Social Policy at Loughborough University. She chairs the Compass management committee was a member of the Commission on Social Justice and the National Equality Panel and is a former director of the Child Poverty Action Group. She has published widely including on poverty and social security.

Dr Mike Phipps is a long-standing member of the editorial board of *Labour Briefing*, a founding member of the Labour Representation Committee (Honorary President: John McDonnell MP) and writes for the website Left Futures. In 2003 he helped set up Iraq Occupation Focus and has edited its fortnightly e-newsletter for several years.

Professor Allyson Pollock is Director of the Institute of Health and Society at Newcastle University and author of *NHS plc: The privatisation of our health care* (Verso Books, 2005).

Dr Glen Rangwala is a lecturer in Middle Eastern politics at Cambridge University. His books include *Iraq in Fragments: The*

Occupation and its Legacy (Hurst, 2006), co-authored with Eric Herring.

Kiri Tunks is Senior Vice President of the National Union of Teachers. She has been a secondary school teacher and trade union activist in London for 24 years and has written widely about education issues.

Hilary Wainwright is a Fellow of the Transnational Institute and co-ordinates the European dimension of its New Politics Project. She is a founder editor and co-editor of *Red Pepper* and author of several books. Her latest is the forthcoming *A New Politics from the Left*.

Chris Williamson MP joined the Labour Party in 1976 and was elected to Parliament in 2010 and again in 2017 after losing his Derby North seat by 41 votes in 2015. He served as shadow fire minister under Ed Miliband for three years and was reappointed to that role by Jeremy Corbyn in July 2017. Before entering Parliament he was a councillor on Derby City Council for 20 years and had two stints as council leader.

ACKNOWLEDGMENTS

The editor wishes to thank all the contributors, all at OR Books and specifically the following for their help in the preparation of this book: Sue Lukes, Liz Davies, Michael Calderbank, Danny Dorling, Kevin Courtney, Jumbo Chan and a number of individuals involved in the 2017 general election campaign who prefer to remain anonymous.

ENDNOTES

INTRODUCTION

1. http://www.huffingtonpost.co.uk/entry/jon-snow-general-election-2017_uk_593b0ee7e4b0240268796496
2. https://www.theguardian.com/politics/2017/apr/27/mugwump-boris-johnson-jeremy-corbyn-mutton-headed-old
3. http://www.counterfire.org/articles/opinion/17807-5-reasons-labour-s-pasokification-has-accelerated
4. See Des Freedland's essay, 'Corbyn Framed and Unframed' in *The Corbyn Effect*, ed. Mark Perryman, Lawrence & Wishart, 2017.
5. https://www.economist.com/news/britain/21723426-labours-leader-has-disrupted-business-politics-jeremy-corbyn-entrepreneur
6. See Íñigo Errejón in conversation with Chantal Mouffe, Podemos: In the name of the people, Soundings Books, 2016.
7. http://www.newstatesman.com/politics/uk/2017/06/they-should-be-bended-knee-apologising-chris-williamson-warns-corbynsceptic
8. Tom Gann, 'Understanding and Building on the Manifesto', https://newsocialist.org.uk/understandingthemanifesto/
9. https://www.theguardian.com/commentisfree/2017/may/16/labour-manifesto-left-election-social-democracy
10. https://www.opendemocracy.net/ourkingdom/stuart-hall-alan-oshea/danger-of-common-sense

ENDNOTES

11. https://www.opendemocracy.net/ourkingdom/stuart-hall-alan-oshea/danger-of-common-sense
12. http://www.progressonline.org.uk/2017/07/12/the-manifesto-wot-won-it/
13. http://www.walesonline.co.uk/news/local-news/jeremy-corbyns-aberdare-talk-among-10917241
14. http://www.huffingtonpost.co.uk/entry/post-brexit-racist-attacks-soar-hate-crimes-reported-to-police-increase-57_uk_57714594e4b08d-2c5639adcb
15. http://lordashcroftpolls.com/wp-content/uploads/2017/06/GE-post-vote-poll-Full-tables.pdf
16. https://www.theguardian.com/commentisfree/2017/may/16/the-guardian-view-on-the-labour-election-manifesto-widening-the-bounds-of-the-thinkable
17. https://www.youtube.com/watch?v=XTll_XH97-4
18. https://www.theguardian.com/commentisfree/2015/sep/13/jeremy-corbyn-labour-leadership-victory-vision
19. http://www.newstatesman.com/politics/uk/2017/06/they-should-be-bended-knee-apologising-chris-williamson-warns-corbynsceptic
20. http://www.progressonline.org.uk/2017/07/12/the-manifesto-wot-won-it/
21. https://www.theguardian.com/politics/2017/jul/01/top-tories-revolt-against-may-public-spending

CHAPTER 1

1. See H. Wainwright and M. Little, *Public Service Reform but Not As We Know it,* published by UNISON and Compass, 2014.
2. Alex Nunns, *The Candidate*, 2016. OR Books.

CHAPTER 2

1. TUC research reported in the Independent, March 12th 2017 http://www.independent.co.uk/news/uk/home-news/one-three-black-asian-minority-ethnic-bame-racism-abuse-assault-brexit-hate-crime-tuc-study-a7634231.html

2. Inquest 2016; and Aadam Muse, Black Lives Matter was not born out of a desire for imitation but of a shared need for liberation, The Independent, August 11th 2016 http://www.independent.co.uk/student/istudents/black-lives-matter-protests-nus-students-uk-london-manchester-whitechapel-demo-march-a7184906.html

3. Jones, Lee. The EU Locked out its people and locked in neoliberalism. Brexit is the Alternative http://blogs.lse.ac.uk/brexit/2016/06/10/the-eu-locked-in-neoliberalism-and-locked-out-its-people-brexit-is-the-alternative/

4. DiEM25 https://diem25.org/

5. *The Independent,* Brexit: People voted to leave because they feared immigration, major study finds, June 28th 2017 http://www.independent.co.uk/news/uk/home-news/brexit-latest-news-leave-eu-immigration-main-reason-european-union-survey-a7811651.html

6. *The Financial Times,* UK areas with most stagnant wages are most anti-EU, June 23rd 2016 https://www.ft.com/content/fe5c6b4e-32f8-11e6-bda0-04585c31b153

7. EMSI, Brexit – How different are the job markets in leave and remain areas?, Duncan Brown, March 27th 2017 https://www.economicmodelling.co.uk/2017/03/27/brexit-different-jobs-markets-leave-remain-areas-2/

8. Who voted for Brexit? How the EU referendum divided generations and social classes, *The Mirror,* June 24th 2016 http://www.mirror.co.uk/news/uk-news/who-voted-brexit-how-eu-8277077 and Revealed: Britain's Deep Divisions In The Brexit Vote, With Education, Race

And Age Key Factors, Huffington Post, February 6th 2017 http://www.huffingtonpost.co.uk/entry/brexit-new-eur-referendum-bbc-analysis-age-race-educational-qualification_uk_58986ffce4b0a1dcbd02faf7

9. Corlett, Adam, The Resolution Foundation, Diverse outcomes: living standards by ethnicity, August 7th 2017 http://www.resolutionfoundation.org/publications/diverse-outcomes-living-standards-by-ethnicity/

10. Wadsworth, Jonathan, Dhingra Swait, Ottaviano Gianmarco, Reenen, Van Reenan, John, Brexit and the Impact of Immigration on the UK, May 11th 2016 http://cep.lse.ac.uk/pubs/download/brexit05.pdf

11. This forms part of my own experience as a union organiser with agency workers in supermarket suppliers, agriculture, aviation services and hospitality industries in the UK between 2005-2016. See also the excellent piece by the General Secretary of the United Voices of the World trade union Petros Elia on this issue of Free Movement and the Posted Workers Directive published by Labour Free Movement, August 2017 https://www.labourfreemovement.org/the-posted-workers-directive-a-red-herring/

12. *The Morning Star,* London strikers unite against trio of bad bosses https://morningstaronline.co.uk/a-fb25-London-strikers-unite-against-trio-of-bad-bosses#.WZwiXFGQzX4

13. Oxford Economics for the British Hospitality Association, The Economic Contribution of the UK Hospitality Industry, September 2015.

14. Williams, Steve, *Introducing Employment Relations*, Third Edition, Oxford University Press, 2014.

15. Trades Union Congress, Still just a bit of banter? August 10th 2016

16. McCluskey, Len, *The Guardian*, December 16th 2016 https://www.theguardian.com/politics/2016/dec/16/len-mccluskey-unite-workers-do-best-when-labour-supply-is-controlled

17. Longdin, Ian, Chartered Institute of Personnel Development, What will Brexit mean for TUPE? June 2nd 2017 https://www.cips.org/supply-management/opinion/2017/june/what-will-brexit-mean-for-tupe/

18. Zahn, Rebecca, Trade Unions, EU workers and 'Brexit': More Complexity, Less Certainty, Manchester Centre for Regulation and Governance, August 15th 2017 http://blog.policy.manchester.ac.uk/posts/2017/08/trade-unions-eu-workers-and-brexit-more-complexity-less-certainty/

19. Bradley, Gracie Mae, Juridified Dispossession: Brexit, Migrant Workers and the Law, Verso blog,December 2nd 2016 https://www.versobooks.com/blogs/2988-juridified-dispossession-brexit-migrant-workers-and-the-law

20. UK Home Office, Residential tenancies provisions of the Immigration Act 2014 (Right to Rent).

21. *Corporatewatch, The Round-Up: rough sleeper immigration raids and charity collaboration*, March 3rd 2017 https://corporatewatch.org/news/2017/mar/05/rough-sleeper-immigration-raids-charity-collaboration-st-mungos-thames-reach

22. North East London Migrant Action, July 2017 https://nelmacampaigns.wordpress.com/

23. Against Borders for Children, FAQ, July 2016 https://www.schoolsabc.net/faqs/

24. Docs Not Cops, FAQ, May 2016 http://www.docsnotcops.co.uk/facts/

25. UK Home Office, Home Office Immigration and Nationality Charges, April 2017.

26. UK Home Office, Migration Advisory Committee, EEA Workers in the UK Labour Market – A briefing note to accompany the call for evidence, August 4th 2017.

27. Anti-trafficking and Labour Exploitation Unit, Briefing for Human Trafficking Foundation on Brexit, September 12th 2016 http://atleu.org.uk/news/2016/9/28/implications-of-brexit-for-victims-of-modern-slavery

28. Kasinof, Laura, Refugees paid one Euro per hour by German employment programme https://codastory.com/migration-crisis/integration-issues/german-employment-program-for-refugees-pays-one-euro-an-hour-sometimes-less

29. European Observatory of Working Life, Denmark: Tripartite agreement on integration of refugees, April 22nd 2016 https://www.eurofound.europa.eu/observatories/eurwork/articles/working-conditions-industrial-relations/denmark-tripartite-agreement-on-integration-of-refugees

30. Kyrewaa, Kojo, Black Lives Matter: crisis shutdown, *Red Pepper*, October 28th 2016 http://www.redpepper.org.uk/crisis-shutdown/

31. Wanjiku Kelbert, Alexandra Climate change is a racist crisis: that's why Black Lives Matter closed an airport, September 6th 2016 https://www.theguardian.com/commentisfree/2016/sep/06/climate-change-racist-crisis-london-city-airport-black-lives-matter

32. Klein, Naomi, Let them drown: The violence of othering in a warming world, *London Review of Books*, June 2nd 2016 https://www.lrb.co.uk/v38/n11/naomi-klein/let-them-drown

33. London's Poverty Profile – London Borough of Kensington and Chelsea 2017 http://www.londonspovertyprofile.org.uk/indicators/boroughs/kensington-and-chelsea/

34. Grenfell Action Group, Blog, June 14th 2017 https://grenfellactiongroup.wordpress.com/2017/06/14/grenfell-tower-fire/ The number of people killed in the fire – currently set at 80 is actually estimated to be twice this number. The occupants of 23 flats are still unaccounted for. The 23 flats which were said to have no survivors were spread between the 11th floor and the 23rd. *Daily Mirror*, Residents in 23 of Grenfell Tower's 129 apartments did not survive the blaze as police say 80 dead, June 28th 2017 http://www.mirror.co.uk/news/uk-news/residents-23-grenfell-towers-129-10703105

35. Take Back Control website https://takebackrealcontrol.com/

36. Momentum, Get Trained Up guide http://www.peoplesmomentum.com/get_trained_up

CHAPTER 3

1. https://www.theguardian.com/education/2016/oct/24/almost-third-of-teachers-quit-within-five-years-of-qualifying-figures

2. DfE – School workforce in England, November 2016 Available at https://www.gov.uk/government/statistics/school-workforce-in-england-november-2016

3. NUT commissioned YouGov poll of 1020 teachers carried out in June/July 2015 and published in October 2015, https://www.teachers.org.uk/news-events/press-releases-england/nutyougov-teacher-survey-government-education-policy

4. National pupil projections: July 2017, https://www.gov.uk/government/statistics/national-pupil-projections-july-2017

5. C Belfield, L Sibieta, Institute for Fiscal Studies, English schools will feel the pinch over the next five years, 21st October 2015 http://www.ifs.org.uk/publications/8027

6. *The Independent*, A-Level courses closed as Michael Gove cuts £100m from sixth form colleges, 3 February 2014, http://www.independent.co.uk/news/education/education-news/exclusive-a-level-courses-closed-as-michael-gove-cuts-100m-from-sixth-form-colleges-9102755.html.

7. DFE – Statistics – national statistics – School Workforce in England: November 2016. Available at https://www.gov.uk/government/statistics/school-workforce-in-england-november-2016

8. https://www.theguardian.com/education/2017/jul/25/more-than-600000-pupils-in-england-taught-by-unqualified-teachers

9. National Union of Teachers, https://www.teachers.org.uk/edufacts/teachers-pay

10. National Union of Teachers, https://www.teachers.org.uk/news-events/press-releases-england/nut-survey-performance-related-pay

11. School Cuts www.schoolcuts.org.uk

12. https://www.tes.com/news/school-news/breaking-news/750000-voters-switched-support-a-result-school-funding-cuts-survey

13. Public Accounts Committee: Establishing free schools, page 15: http://www.publications.parliament.uk/pa/cm201314/cmselect/cmpubacc/941/941.pdf(14) https://www.theguardian.com/education/2015/jan/27/no-proof-academies-raise-standards-education-inquiry

14. National Audit Office, Capital funding for schools (22 February 2017). Available at: https://www.nao.org.uk/report/capital-funding-for-schools/

16. National Audit Office: Financial Sustainability of Schools, December 2016: https://www.nao.org.uk/report/financial-sustainability-in-schools/

17. Hansard, 18th July 2017, https://hansard.parliament.uk/Commons/2017-07-18/debates/733C6229-49D0-4559-8F59-5F1244C-2DE13/DrugsPolicy#contribution-B9E0C405-B5B5-4B38-9EA4-966E4C0A079F

18. National Union of Teachers, 12th February 2016, https://www.teachers.org.uk/news-events/press-releases-england/teachers-question-accuracy-of-baseline-assessment-atl-nut-survey

19. Hutchings, Merryn, *Exam Factories?,* July 2015, https://www.teachers.org.uk/education-policies/research/examfactories

20. https://www.theguardian.com/education/2015/may/14/calls-to-child-line-over-exam-stress-break-records

21. UNICEF Office of Research (2013), Child Well-being in Rich Countries: A Comparative Overview. Innocenti Report Card 11, Florence: UNICEF Office of Research. Available at: http://www.unicef-irc.org/publications/pdf/rc11_eng.pdf

CHAPTER 4

1. The Institute of Employment Rights is a think tank for the labour movement and a charity. It exists to inform the debate around union rights and labour law by providing information, critical analysis and policy ideas through our network of academics, researchers and lawyers. It was established in 1989 as an independent organisation to act as a focal point for the spread of new ideas in the field of labour law. In 1994, the Institute became a registered charity. See http://www.ier.org.uk/ for its list of activities and publications.

2. The detailed proposals can be found at https://www.tuc.org.uk/workplace-issues/employment-rights/proposed-changes-law/trade-union-freedom-bill/proposal-trade and https://www.tuc.org.uk/employment-rights/trade-union-freedom-bill/trade-union-freedom-bill-explanatory-notes

CHAPTER 6

1. The discussion herein mainly focuses on housing policy in England as housing is a devolved matter albeit in different ways for Scotland, Wales and Northern Ireland.

2. The Conservative Government is currently consulting on ending such practices for new owners, but there is as yet no proposal to extend this retrospectively to existing leases.

CHAPTER 7

1. https://www.pwc.com/gx/en/banking-capital-markets/publications/assets/pdf/next-chapter-creating-understanding-of-spvs.pdf

2. See for example: http://www.pulsetoday.co.uk/news/commissioning/how-the-nhs-is-spending-millions-on-consultancy-firms/20035171.

article and https://www.bma.org.uk/news/2017/june/doctors-horrified-by-staff-costs

3. http://www.nottinghampost.com/news/health/controversial-firm-capita-handed-27m-377493

4. https://calderdaleandkirklees999callforthenhs.wordpress.com/2017/09/01/buyer-beware-centene-corporation-contract-with-nottingham-nhs-organisations-is-2-7m-can-of-worms/

5. https://chpi.org.uk/papers/reports/pfi-profiting-from-infirmaries/

6. https://publications.parliament.uk/pa/cm201617/cmselect/cmpubacc/887/88702.htm

7. http://www.nhsforsale.info/private-provders/private-provider-profiles-2/hca.html

8. See for example: http://www.hempsons.co.uk/news/strategic-estates-partnerships-investing-challenging-times-briefing/

9. https://www.hsj.co.uk/finance-and-efficiency/exclusive-private-deals-being-planned-to-release-naylor-billions/7018691.article

10. http://www.gponline.com/bma-urges-caution-developers-of-fer-33bn-primary-care-premises-overhaul/article/1441684

11. LaingBuisson, Primary Care & Out-Of-Hospital Services, Second Edition, 2015).

12. https://www.hsj.co.uk/finance-and-efficiency/exclusive-naylor-delighted-at-33bn-private-investment-offer/7020346.article

13. https://www.parliament.uk/business/committees/committees-a-z/commons-select/public-accounts-committee/inquiries/parliament-2015/financial-sustainability-nhs-16-17/

14. www.nhsbill2015.org

15. https://www.thetimes.co.uk/article/a-spoonful-of-competition-is-ordered-to-revitalise-nhs-b3hgvdpfgmg

16. https://publications.parliament.uk/pa/cm201012/cmselect/cmhealth/1431/1431we06.htm and https://publications.parliament.uk/pa/cm201011/cmselect/cmhealth/796/79611.htm

17. http://press.labour.org.uk/post/151047163644/diane-abbott-mp-shad-ow-secretary-of-state-for/embed

CHAPTER 8

1. https://www.theguardian.com/commentisfree/2017/mar/31/labour-leadership-jeremy-corbyn-tom-watson

2. V3.co.uk: Crime is moving online as cyber and fraud incidents soar. October 2015 http://www.v3.co.uk/v3-uk/news/2430617/crime-is-moving-online-as-cyber-and-fraud -incidents-soar

3. JRF Poverty and Crime Review. May 2014 http://eprints.lancs. ac.uk/71188/1/JRF_Final_Poverty_and_Crime_Review_May_2014.pdf

4. http://www.telegraph.co.uk/comment/personal-view/3622123/Daddy-Cameron-knows-whats-best.html

5. Daily Telegraph: Private companies in hospitals, police and schools are here to stay. 1st March 2012 http://www.telegraph.co.uk/news/9116667/Private-companies-in-hospitals-police-and-schools-are-here-to-stay-says-Oliver-Letwin.html

6. Institute for Criminal Policy Research: Highest to Lowest-Prison Population http://www.prisonstudies.org/highest-to-lowest/prison_population_rate?field_region_taxonomy_tid=14

7. Ministry of Justice: Costs per place and costs per prisoner. 29 October 2015 https://www.gov.uk/government/uploads/system/uploads/attachment_data/file/471625/costs-per-place.pdf

8. Criminal Justice and Courts Bill – Fact sheet: Secure Colleges https://www.gov.uk/government/uploads/system/uploads/attachment_data/file/322165/fact-sheet-secure-colleges.pdf

9. Eton College: School Fees – 2015/2016 http://www.etoncollege.com/CurrentFees.aspx

10. Centre for Crime and Justice Studies: The Troubled Families Programme: the perfect social policy? November 2015 http://www.crimeandjustice.

org.uk/sites/crimeandjustice.org.uk/files/The%20Troubled%20Families%20Programme,%20Nov%202015.pdf

11. *The Guardian*: Troubled families scheme outcomes: miraculous success or pure fiction? 22 June 2015 http://www.theguardian.com/politics/2015/jun/22/troubled-families-scheme-outcomes-miraculous-success-or-pure-fiction

12. http://truepublica.org.uk/united-kingdom/privatising-britains-immigration-service-5-48-send-email/

13. https://grenfellactiongroup.wordpress.com/2016/11/20/kctmo-playing-with-fire/

CHAPTER 9

1. https://www.theguardian.com/local-government-network/2011/aug/12/participatory-budgeting-localism-big-society

CHAPTER 10

1. Ministry of Justice, *The Governance of Britain* (The Stationary Office, London: 2007).

2. Dworkin, Ronald, *A Bill of Rights for Britain* (Chatto and Windus, London: 1990), pp. 35-6.

3. Op. cit., p. 55.

4. Beetham, David, *Unelected Oligarchy: Corporate and Financial Dominance in Britain's Democracy* (Democratic Audit, Liverpool: 2011); also available freely online.

5. Shaxson, Nicholas, *Treasure Islands: Tax Havens and the Men Who Stole the World* (The Bodley Head, London: 2011).

6. A thorough analysis of different electoral systems according to democratic criteria can be found in Chapter 9, 'Democratic Criteria for Electoral Systems' in Beetham, David, *Democracy and Human Rights* (Polity Press, Cambridge: 1999, pp. 170 – 194).

CHAPTER 11

1. https://www.theguardian.com/society/2017/jan/06/nhs-faces-humanitarian-crisis-rising-demand-british-red-cross
2. https://www.theguardian.com/housing-network/2015/nov/06/cuts-womens-refuges-violence-death-social-housing
3. http://www.independent.co.uk/news/uk/politics/theresa-may-immigration-target-queens-speech-net-migration-cap-not-mentioned-a7801721.html
4. http://www.mirror.co.uk/news/politics/tory-benefit-cuts-today-disability-10144250
5. https://www.theguardian.com/careers/2017/may/22/cruel-and-humiliating-why-fit-for-work-tests-are-failing-people-with-disabilities
6. http://www.aljazeera.com/news/2017/02/uk-hate-crime-record-levels-brexit-vote-170215123414863.html
7. https://www.opensocietyfoundations.org/sites/default/files/eroding-trust-20161017_0.pdf
8. https://www.theguardian.com/uk-news/2017/jul/17/manchester-mosque-left-gutted-after-suspected-arson-attack
9. http://www.bbc.co.uk/news/uk-england-london-40632161
10. http://www.independent.co.uk/news/uk/home-news/four-year-old-raises-concerns-of-radicalisation-after-pronouncing-cucumber-as-cooker-bomb-a6927341.html
11. https://inews.co.uk/essentials/news/environment/anti-fracking-campaigners-labelled-extremists-efforts-stop-terrorists/
12. *Tell it Like it is: How Our Schools Fail Black Children* (2005).
13. http://www.telegraph.co.uk/comment/personal-view/3639448/Poor-Britannia-10-awful-years-under-Blairism.html
14. http://news.bbc.co.uk/1/hi/uk/2765041.stm
15. *Punishing the Poor: The Neoliberal Government of Social Insecurity* (Politics, History, and Culture) Paperback (2009).

16. http://conservativehome.blogs.com/centreright/2008/04/making-history.html and http://www.independent.co.uk/news/uk/politics/margaret-thatchers-legacy-spilt-milk-new-labour-and-the-big-bang-she-changed-everything-8564541.html

17. https://www.theguardian.com/education/2009/apr/23/students-condemn-lecturers-strike

18. http://www.telegraph.co.uk/news/politics/labour/11532277/manifesto-2015-summary.html

19. http://www.newstatesman.com/politics/2015/03/labours-anti-immigrant-mug-worst-part-it-isnt-gaffe

20. http://www.independent.co.uk/news/uk/politics/generalelection/ed-miliband-unveils-stone-carved-with-labour-pledges-to-be-placed-at-downing-st-if-he-wins-10221946.html

21. http://www.refuge.org.uk/get-help-now/what-is-domestic-violence/domestic-violence-the-facts/

22. https://www.nusconnect.org.uk/articles/no-police-in-pride-no-pride-in-the-police https://www.rt.com/uk/209287-london-protest-ferguson-solidarity/

23. http://www.defendtherighttoprotest.org/ferguson-solidarity-tour-uk-2015/

24. https://www.theguardian.com/uk-news/2015/sep/12/london-rally-solidarity-with-refugees

25. https://www.theguardian.com/us-news/video/2017/jan/30/thousands-protest-trump-muslim-ban-london-video

26. https://www.theguardian.com/uk-news/2016/oct/19/uks-prevent-counter-radicalisation-policy-badly-flawed and http://www.independent.co.uk/voices/letters/prevent-will-have-a-chilling-effect-on-open-debate-free-speech-and-political-dissent-10381491.html 6

27. https://www.theguardian.com/politics/2016/aug/28/corbyn-accuses-labour-officials-of-suspending-party-members-without-explanation and https://www.theguardian.com/politics/2016/aug/26/pro-corbyn-union-leader-threatens-legal-action-over-labour-suspension